Gozo, Malta Environmental History
People, Culture, Tradition, Travel and tourism

Author
Eugene Hext

Copyright Notice

Copyright © 2017 Global Print Digital
All Rights Reserved

Digital Management Copyright Notice. This Title is not in public domain, it is copyrighted to the original author, and being published by **Global Print Digital**. No other means of reproducing this title is accepted, and none of its content is editable, neither right to commercialize it is accepted, except with the consent of the author or authorized distributor. You must purchase this Title from a vendor who's right is given to sell it, other sources of purchase are not accepted, and accountable for an action against. We are happy that you understood, and being guided by these terms as you proceed. Thank you

First Printing: 2017.

ISBN: 978-1-912483-44-0

Publisher: Global Print Digital.
Arlington Row, Bibury, Cirencester GL7 5ND
Gloucester
United Kingdom.
Website: www.homeworkoffer.com

.

Table of Content

INTRODUCTION 1
HISTORY 5
HISTORY AND HERITAGE LINKING MALTA AND GOZO 19
GOZO 39
TRAVEL AND TOURISM 48
THE SISTER ISLES 48
WHAT TO SEE AND DO 50
Archaeological Sites 52
Churches & Religious Sites 59
Boat Diving 66
Shore Diving 68
Diving Centres 73
Fortifications & Towers 82
Museums & Galleries 84
Natural Attractions 92
Shopping 97
Facilitie 102
Service Providers 103
Theatre & Opera 109
Towns & Villages 110
Visitor Attractions 130
Restaurants 133
Vineyards 146
Wedding Venues 149
GOZO EVENTS 152
MEET IN GOZO 152
COMINO 154

Introduction

About the Sister Isle
Gozo meaning "joy" in Castilian, is the second largest Island of the Maltese archipelago, with a population of approximately 30,000.

Though separated from mainland Malta by a mere 5km stretch of sea, Gozo is distinctly different from Malta. The Island is a third the size of Malta, more rural and tranquil. Its culture and way of life are rooted in tradition and yet open to the present.

Exuding a relaxed pace of life, Gozo is the ideal secluded haven and at just 25 minutes or so by ferry from Malta, the hop can easily be made for even the shortest stay.

For well over two millennia, life in Gozo was harsh, as the island was left exposed to any passing raiders, much more so than Malta with its natural harbours and defences. Throughout the Middle Ages and into the rule of the Knights, Barbary corsairs and Saracens raided the island at intervals. In 1551, the latter carried out a devastating raid, taking almost the entire population away into slavery. The island never really recovered from this and remained under populated for centuries, until the arrival of the Knights saw the medieval Citadel in what is now Victoria refortified and the Gozitans began to venture down to the rest of the Island.

Gozo and its inhabitants have their own distinct character and identity, with noticeably different lifestyles, accents and dialect. Gozitans are known for their friendliness and warm welcome, going out of their way to help a visitor find their destination.

Festas and carnival times in Gozo also have a different feel to those on Malta. The village of Nadur celebrates carnival with a black sense of humour, quite unlike its more joyful counterparts elsewhere.

The real beauty of Gozo, apart from its stunning seascape and interior, lies in the villages. Here, it seems as if time really stood still. The locals treasure their peace and the villages are tranquil, providing a wonderful respite from the modern pace that many of the city dwellers have to endure in their everyday life.

All roads in Gozo lead to Victoria, also known as Rabat, which is where the fortified citadel sits atop a summit. Victoria is not just the geographic heart of Gozo, but also the centre of everyday activity. It manages to combine the bustle of its market and shops with a relaxed and sociable atmosphere. It is a great place to watch the islanders go about their day, especially when the main market square, It-Tokk, comes to life. The town also has a thriving cultural life all its own, with some surprising attractions ranging from opera to horse races in the main street on festa day.

Gozo is well served by restaurants, where the eating is good and varied. Apart from restaurants and cafés offering local dishes, as well as continental menus, one can also enjoy restaurants specialising in ethnic cuisines, such as Chinese or Indian. You will be spoilt for choice in Rabat, Mgarr and the resort towns of Marsalforn and Xlendi, as well as in several other places around the island.

You will find that it is comfortable to walk about at any time of day or night. The sense of safety and security is tangible as the locals take pride in the absolute absence of serious crime and the almost non-existence of theft.

Where to Stay

For a taste of village life, rent a villa or farmhouse, and a taste of luxury, rent one with a pool. Other accommodation ranges from deluxe hotels to self-catering apartments. Sea or country views are never hard to find in Gozo, wherever you choose to stay.

History

Malta is situated in the middle of the Mediterranean Sea, halfway between Gibraltar and Alexandria, and Sicily and North Africa. Thus it has always been at the cross-roads of the trading and warring routes of this land-locked sea.

Malta is chiefly composed of limestone with no hills higher than 300 metres and no rivers. On the South-West side it is guarded by high cliffs whilst on the North-East side the shore is indented with sheltered harbours. These proved to be very attractive to the sailors and navigators that sailed the Mediterranean.

The origin of Maltese history goes back to some 4500 years BC, when some people from the neighbouring island of Sicily, who could see the island lying on the horizon, decided to cross the narrow waters to investigate. This obviously could not have happened unless these people had skills in sailing or rowing some form of craft which was large enough to carry with them their belongings, which included such animals as sheep, goats and cattle, as well as seeds like wheat and barley.

These people settled on the island and sheltered in the many caves which exist there. The earliest inhabited cave is called 'Ghar-Dalam', the cave of darkness, where remains of these people and their artefacts give us an insight into their way of life. They cultivated the land, growing wheat and barley and practised animal husbandry.

Around 3500 BC they started to build large buildings the like of which were not to be found anywhere else. They kept in touch with their cousins in Sicily obtaining from them obsidian and flint with which they could make tools to help them work the stones. These buildings, of which there are fifteen , are spread across the island. They are the oldest existing megalithic structures known to man - places like Hagar Qim, Mnajdra, Tarxien, etc. antedate the pyramids and Stonehenge by some 1000 years. This Neolithic peril about 1800 years, when, for no explicable reason, it ended abruptly. Nobody knows what happened, but famine, over population and disease could have been possible causes.

Around 1200 BC Phoenicia started to expand her empire. The Phoenicians were traders and great mariners who sailed their ships along the shores of the Mediterranean. They sailed to England where they traded tin. It is said that they circumnavigated the continent of Africa. They settled on the North coast of Africa and established a city called Carthage. They also settled on the West coast of Sicily and in Malta. Indeed, the name 'Malta' is said to be derived from the Phoenician word 'Maleth', meaning refuge. Their stay in Malta was to last for 320 years. Conceivably the roots of the Maltese language derive from this Phoenician period. The Phoenicians also introduced glass making and weaving and built temples were they could worship their gods.

Meanwhile, the city of Carthage grew in size and strength and eventually carved out an empire which covered the North African coast to the west of Carthage, and included Spain, Sardinia, Western Sicily and Malta. The Carthaginians got into difficulties with the Greeks in Eastern Sicily and with the arrival of Rome on the political scene during the 3rd century BC it was inevitable that the two nations would wage war for mastery of the area. Three wars, known as the Punic Wars, were fought from 264 to 146 BC ending with the fall of Carthage, and with Rome becoming supreme in the Central and Western Mediterranean. Malta became part of the Roman Empire during the 2nd Punic War (c. 218 BC) and remained part of the empire till the Vandals raided the islands in AD 395. One event of great importance to the Maltese took place in AD 5 8, when St. Paul, who was on his way to Rome as a prisoner, was shipwrecked on the Island. He stayed for three months during which time he introduced Christianity to the people. The Maltese take great pride in saying that they were one of the first nations to accept Christianity as their faith - but that is another story.

We now enter a dark period in Maltese history, the period from AD 395 to 535. No records exist as to what happened during that time. Rome fell the Vandals in AD 455 and it is quite likely that towards the end of the 4th century, Malta too became part of the Ostrogothic Kingdom centred in Rome In AD 535, Malta was conquered by General Belissarius the Byzantine to form part of the Eastern Roman or Byzantine Empire, till the arrival of the Arabs.

Islam started with the Hegira, when Mohammed fled from Mecca to Medina in AD 622. Before long his followers spread across North Africa into Spain and across the Pyrenees. Their expansion into Europe was stopped by the French King Charles Martel at Tours in AD 732, just one hundred years after the death of Mohammed. They invaded and captured Palermo in AD 832 and in 870 they invaded Malta. Once again Malta came in contact with a new and vigorous Semitic people.

Unfortunately, very little documentation relating to the two centuries of Arab rule in Malta survives today. Indeed, Arab influence in Malta lasted much longer, since the Normans, who invaded in 1090 and took over the island from the Arabs, were indeed enlightened people and they tolerated the presence of the Arabs in the island. In fact, Count Roger never garrisoned the islands. Arab influence remained more or less unrestricted till about 1224, when the Muslims were finally expelled. The chief legacy of the Arab occupation in Malta must be the Maltese language itself, which has many elements of Arabic.

Legends about the coming of Count Roger and the Normans to Malta are numerous, but most probably unfounded. Count Roger is said to have given Malta her flag based on the Hauteville colours. He is reputed to have re-Christianised the Maltese, established churches, re-appointed a bishop and even expelled the Arabs. All of this is doubtful. However, the Normans' presence opened the door for the re-Europeanisation of the Maltese people. The so-called Norman Period lasted till 1194 and though the Normans left many treasures and architecture in Sicily, hardly any relics of this period exist in Malta.

Following the death of King Roger II in 1154, a series of political struggles ensued. William the Good died childless in 1189 and a dispute arose over his successor. The rightful heir was the daughter of Roger 1, Constance, who was married to Henry VI, son of the German Emperor, Frederick Barbarossa. However, the Pope had other ideas. Fearing the penetration of the Germans in Sicily and Southern Italy, the church threw its support with Tancred. He was crowned king in 1190. However, he did not last long because Henry VI, through a series of intrigues within Tancred's court, acquired Sicily in 1194. Thus Malta became part of the German Kingdom under Frederick II - the Hohenstaufen rule. The Arabs were finally expelled from Sicily and Malta after an uprising in 1224.

Following the death of Frederick II in 1250, the Hohenstaufen dynasty declined very rapidly. Many of Frederick's enemies, including the church, were keen to rid Sicily and Southern Italy of the Germans. Sixteen years of plots and counterplots eventually brought a new master to Malta. In 1266, Pope Clement finally achieved his objective and proclaimed Charles of Anjou as King of Sicily.

Although the period of Angevin rule over Malta was short-lived (1266-1283), it is from this point onward that Malta shifted into the

European scheme of government and administration. Because of high taxation, moves were made in Sicily to restore the island to Aragon, the rightful heirs to the crown of Sicily. Things came to a head in 1282 with the Sicilian uprising against the French, known as the Sicilian Vespers, which led to a bloody massacre of the French. The Aragonese took immediate advantage and installed Peter of Aragon as ruler of Sicily and Malta.

The Aragonese period in Malta was to last for 130 years. During that time the Maltese people suffered the indignity of having their island handed from one noble to another as a fief for various services rendered to the king. These individuals increased taxation which led to local unrest amongst the people. Malta remained at the mercy of these powerful Sicilian magnates, like the Alagonas and the Moncadas. It was not till 1397 that the local council for Malta and Gozo, the Universita, made a strong petition to the crown for the islands to be restored to direct rule by the King.

In 1412, Ferdinand de Antequera was elected King of Aragon, Castille and Sicily, the first Castillian to ever occupy the throne. In 1421, King Alfonso granted the Maltese islands and all the revenue from them to Don Antonio Cardona in exchange for a loan of 30,000 gold florins. He then transferred his right over Malta and Gozo to

Don Gonsalvo Monroy. The Maltese disagreed with this arrangement. After five years they finally rebelled. In 1426 they pillaged Monroy's house in Mdina and laid siege to his castle at Birgu. The Maltese bought back the island for 30,000 florins. They also insisted on radical reforms including one that said that the islands wore never to be ceded again by the crown. Alfonso agreed to these reforms and finally ratified them in a Royal Charter in 1428.

In 1479, Ferdinand II married Isabella of Castille. Their daughter Joanna married Philip Archduke of Austria. In 1518, the Habsburg dynasty was consolidated when their son Charles V, became the Holy Roman Emperor. Through the intercession of Pope Clement VIII, he granted Malta, Gozo and Tripoli to the homeless Order of St. John in 1530.

The Order of St. John came to Malta after the loss of Rhodes in 1522. They had been in Rhodes since 1309. Before that they were in the Holy Land where the Order was established in 1099 by Blessed Gerard to look after the pilgrims and the crusaders. The main enemy now was Turkey. The Ottomans were the dread of the Christian powers bordering the Mediterranean and the Balkans. Malta was becoming of supreme strategic importance for the control of the Mediterranean against the alarming growth of

Muslim power. In 1547 the Turks made an unexpected attack on Malta and Gozo, taking many prisoners. The attack that followed in 1551 was more serious, for they ransacked Gozo and made off with 5000 prisoners. The Order was convinced that they must prepare the defences of the island for a bigger invasion. Soon afterwards, in 1565, a great Turkish armada appeared off the coast of Malta, starting what is now called The Great Siege of Malta, which was to last for four long months. When it was finally raised on the 7th September of the same year, many knights and Maltese had lost their lives, as did many Turks.

After the siege a new city was built, called Valletta in honour of the Grand Master who led the Order through the siege. This was to be a modem, fortified city, and eventually a city of culture and commerce. The city grew and so did the wealth of the Order. The threat of Turkish invasion was ever present. In 1572 the Turkish fleet was defeated by the Christian powers, including the Order, led by Don Juan of Austria at the battle of Lepanto.

In the years that followed, Valletta became an impregnable fortress, housing imposing palaces and churches. It also became a flourishing centre for trade and learning. Successive Grandmasters initiated grand projects, such as the building of many fortifications, aqueducts and a university, where the teaching of anatomy and surgery took place.

As time went by, however, the Order began to decline. The haughtiness and despotism of some of the Grandmasters upset the Maltese, leading to the famous Rebellion of the Priests, led by Mannarino in 1775 during the magistery of Ximenes de Texada. After the death of Grandmaster de Rohan (1797) the Order elected Ferdinand von Hompesch as its leader.

The situation in Europe at the time was explosive. The French revolution had changed the face of Europe and through the influence of Napoleon Bonaparte, 'The Directory' gave him permission to invade Egypt and take Malta in the process. In 1798 he invaded Malta and expelled the Order. Thus ended 268 years of rule by the Order of St. John.

French rule in Malta lasted only two years. The Maltese rebelled within three months of their arrival, besieging them in Valletta, from where, with the help of the British, they were finally ousted in 1800. The British occupied the island and for the next fifteen years the fate of Malta was undecided. The Maltese did not want the knights back and Britain was quite undecided as to whether it wanted to stay in Malta, but equally Britain did not want either the

French or the Russians, who had their eyes on Malta for quite a while, to occupy the islands. The Maltese finally made up their mind and asked the British to stay. In the treaty of Paris, the occupation of Malta by the British was finally recognised. This was legalised in 1815 at the Congress of Vienna.

The Maltese got used to British rule but it was not long before the Maltese appealed to the British for equal participation in the running of their island. Mitrovich and Sceberras made extraordinary efforts for this cause, as a result of which a Council of Government was set up in 1835, a small beginning along the road to representative government.

Despite slow progress in the field of constitutional reform, Malta moved ahead, particularly in defence and imperial strategy. Malta benefited from increased defence spending by Britain. The dockyards were enlarged with five new dry docks being completed by 187 1. Malta prospered.

The Crimean War (1854-56) again brought considerable military activity to the island and Malta's importance as a supply station and as a naval base was unquestionable. When steam replaced sails, and after the opening of the Suez canal, Malta thrived. She was now on the highway between Europe and the East. With every ship calling, the grand harbour became a beehive of activity from which everybody benefited.

As usual the island's prosperity was quickly reflected in a dramatic rise in the population. This would continue well into the 20th century. From 114,000 in 1842, the population rose to 124,000 by 1851. Twenty years later it would reach 140,000 and it would more than double by the advent of World War II. With each increase, the problem of congestion, especially in the urban areas of Valletta and the Three Cities, would become serious. Attempts were made to encourage the people to move to the newer suburbs and the older towns and villages. Despite the prosperity, employment for the ever increasing work force would not always be available. Emigration schemes were introduced which initially were not successful. However, towards the end of the century, with the trade boom on the decline and Malta's fortune ebbing, the Maltese started to emigrate, mainly to North Africa.

The political situation in Malta before World War I was increasingly overshadowed by the economic gloom that engulfed the island. The position deteriorated over a long time due to competition from other well-equipped ports in the Mediterranean. Government revenue from the slower activities in Malta's ports was falling steeply. It became clear that Malta's dependence on Britain's military spending was a severe handicap. Whenever there was a cut in defence spending, the people suffered.

The winds of change in Europe and the gathering clouds of war also weighed heavily over Malta, and when World War I broke out, the people rallied to the allied cause. The naval dockyards again came into their own - but at the close of the war Malta had to once more face reality. There were to be severe cutbacks in defence spending. Much hardship and distress followed. Men were discharged from the army and naval establishments, unemployment soared and inflation ate its way into the miserable pay packets. There were strikes and protests. On the 7th June 1919 a huge and angry crowd gathered in Valletta for one of the meetings of the assembly. The pent-up frustration of the people suddenly exploded into a riot. The mob got out of control and caused much damage. Troops were called in and they opened fire. Five men were killed.

In 1921 Malta achieved responsible government. Under a new constitution she was to have a legislative assembly composed of 32 elected members and an upper house of 16 members. All internal domestic affairs were to be in the hands of the Maltese with Britain retaining responsibility for foreign affairs and defence.

Germany started the Second World War in September 1939. Malta was soon in the thick of it, once again coveted for its great strategic position in the Mediterranean. She was bombed very heavily by the Italian and German air forces and after two and a half years of never-ending air raids, the bravery, heroism and sacrifice of its people were recognised when King George VI awarded the Maltese people the George Cross Medal.

After the war Britain started the process of decolonisation. Malta too was part of that process, but her path to independence was slow and often uncertain. Self-government was restored in 1947, but the decision of the British Government to dismiss workers from the dockyards caused massive unemployment. Consequently, there began a great exodus of Malta's people to the United States, Canada and Australia, where work was available.

By 1964 a call for independence was made by the major political parties and after discussions with the British Government, an independence agreement, tied to a ten year defence and financial accord with the United Kingdom was finally approved. On 21 September 1964, Malta became a sovereign and independent nation within the Commonwealth.

Ten years later, Parliament enacted important changes to the constitution and on the 13th December 1974, Malta was declared a Republic within the Commonwealth and appointed Sir Anthony Mamo as the first Maltese President of the Republic of Malta. Five years later, the last of the British troops on the island left Malta and on 31 March 1979 the Union Jack was finally lowered. Malta had at last reached the goal for which its people had striven for many centuries - the ability to make decisions on their own for their own good and the good of their own people, without any interference from outside powers. Malta is represented at the United Nations, takes an active part in European affairs and has finally taken its rightful place amongst the nations of the world.

History and Heritage linking Malta and Gozo

The lack of sufficient documents sometimes causes the Mediaeval history of Malta and Gozo to seem obscure. History, especially that of the Middle Ages, has to be compiled from what is to be found in the written document of that period. In the case of our islands the majority of documents have been lost or destroyed during the course of the centuries. What has survived the vicissitudes of various dominations, neglect through ignorance and wholesale destruction in times of plague, are to be found in archives and libraries often far apart which makes research considerably difficult.

In Malta a few important documents concerning the late Middle Ages are preserved in the Royal Library in Valletta, and some others are in the archives of the Metropolitan Cathedral at Notabile. In the island of Gozo, so far, no documents have been found relating to the Middle Ages, in fact the earliest manuscript volume kept among the archives of the Università del Gozo and preserved in the Public Library at Victoria, Gozo, is dated 1560-1592.

In the archives of Palermo, Messina, Catania and Naples, other documents concerning the Middle Ages of Malta and Gozo are to be found. We can safely presume that some documents of that period and relating to Malta and Gozo are to be found at the Vatican Library. Fortunately through the research of scholars interesting documents relating directly or indirectly to both islands are occasionally published abroad, and through these erudite works we are given a glimpse of much we would wish to know. Such a work was published in Palermo in 1918, by Doctors Salvatore Giambruno and Luigi Genuardi. The work is entitled CAPITOLI INEDITI DELLE CITTÁ DEMANIALI DI SICILIA, APPROVATI SINO AL 1458. Among the other crown lands treated in this work are the island of Gozo on pages 323-335, and the island of Malta on pages 375-423.

There is a copy of this rare work on the shelves of the Royal Library in Valletta, bearing the following press mark CD. 3. 34. As this article is relating to Gozo we shall deal solely with that part of the work referring to the Capitoli of Gozo.

We shall now attempt to give a brief introduction to the sister isle in mediaeval times. The island of Gozo suffered the same vicissitudes as the island of Malta. As far back as we can go we find that both islands were given as a fief to feudal lords. As stated by Giambruno and Genuardi both islands had changed hands many times being given in fief to Margaritone of Brindisi, grand admiral of Sicily; to Guglielmo Grasso, another admiral; to the Infante Giovanni, duke of Athens and Neopatria; then to his son Infante Federico; to Guglielmo and later to Luigi of Aragon; to Guglielmo Raimondo Moncada; and to Don Artale d'Alagona.

Normally a royal fief was enjoyed by the possessor for as long as he, or his heirs, survived. When, however, the possessor forfeited the fief either through rebellious conduct or behaviour unworthy of the trust placed in him by his sovereign, then the land reverted to the overlord, to be conferred on another favourite.

This constant change of masters and ignoble position was much disliked by the inhabitants of both islands. The people petitioned King Ludovico of Sicily to integrate Malta and Gozo to his crown lands in such a way as no longer would it be possible for either to be donated in fief. In a charter dated 7th October, 1350, King Ludovico granted this petition, though the privilege of being directly under the King was ignored. The usefulness of these islands as a means of rewarding service was too great for the king to renounce. However, when Guglielmo Raimondo Moncada forfeited the fief through high treason, in 1397 king Martin of Sicily fully integrated Malta and Gozo to his crown property. In 1398 the Parliament of Syracuse met to formulate a list of the towns considered as cities of the crown, and in this list we find the islands of Malta and Gozo.

Under the rule of Alfonso, king of Aragon and Sicily, Malta and Gozo were again given as fief in 1420, this time for 30,000 florins to Antonio Cardona, Viceroy of Sicily. In 1425 king Alfonso once more conceded the islands, also for 30,000 florins to Don Consalvo Monroy.

The inhabitants of both islands were sorely tried at this treatment and sent a ambassadors to Spain requesting that their homeland be redeemed and returned to the crown, and that all their forfeited privileges be respected as erstwhile. On the 20th June, 1428, the Maltese and Gozitans redeemed these islands by paying 80,000 florins, for which act the king promised that in future both islands were to remain an integral part of his kingdom. In parenthesis we can say that this promise was honoured until 1530, when Malta and Gozo were donated to the Knights of St. John of Jerusalem.

Gozo, ever proud of its ancient privileges, jealously guarded its rights — in fact we find that Gozo had its own government: Consiglio Popolare framed on the form of government in Malta. The titles of the various officiais were identical: Capitano della Verga, Giurati, Judges, Catapani, Marammero, etc. Gozo had its own Consuls in Sicily and these dealt directly with the king's representative in Sicily.

We find that petitions were sent by the government of Malta and Gozo separately, either to the king or to the viceroy in Sicily. These petitions were called "capitoli" and the sovereign, or the viceroy, reserved the right to approve or reject, or adjust them according to circumstances. There are some instances when Malta and Gozo petitioned jointly, thus in a capitolo of 1427 we read: li presenti capituli si intendanu tantu per la insola di Malta quanto di Gozu.

The first capitolo mentioned in the book under review relating solely to Gozo is dated at Messina, 31st October, 1432, XI Indiction. The original was written in siculo-latin from which is made the following precis.

Petitioners asked the king to show them clemency. On account of a recent moorish invasion in which great devastation had taken place through destruction of their cattle and crops, they would not be able to harvest grain and other crops, therefore they beseeched the king to decree that they would be allowed to obtain the necessary provisions from Sicily without taxation.

The second clause of this capitolo deals with the importation of cattle. The Gozitans, requested exemption from taxation on the importation of livestock, pleading that with the money thus saved they would be enabled to purchase provisions necessary for the population.

In the third clause they begged for an exemption of fine and punishment for the offence of gambling, pleading that by making gambling illegal the population were falling into more pernicious and hazardous games.

The fourth clause asks for a moratorium on account of the Moorish invasion.

The fifth clause of this capitolo deals with the elections of government officials. It was petitioned that no longer would the officials be elected by favouritism, and that the Giurati, the Treasurer, the Catapani and Judges of the Civil Court of Gozo together with its Notary be elected in a fair manner.

In the sixth clause they petitioned that no longer would a commissioner be sent from Sicily to decide certain cases in the civil court of Gozo. They stated that on the answer to this petition being favourable they would boycott any foreign commissioner inadvertently sent to Gozo.

In the seventh clause they beseeched the king to reconfirm their ancient privileges, capitoli, freedoms, etc., granted either written or unwritten.

In the eighth clause the Gozitans submitted that the post of Capitan della Verga be conferred on a Gozitan, pleading that among their ranks were many a man worthy of occupying this post. They asked that a foreigner might not be allowed to occupy this position any longer.

The ninth clause also refers to the Capitan della Verga. They asked that the term of office should be for the period of a year, notwithstanding any concession or understanding promised for an extension of the term of office.

In the tenth clause they petitioned that grain harvested from lands belonging to the crown should not be exported from Gozo, but stored on the island for emergency. The reply to this particular clause is interesting and therefore it is included. It was granted that grain grown in Gozo would be for the use of the Gozitans. However, when the harvest was superabundant, then the surplus would be exported to Malta for the use of the citizen and inhabitants of that island.

The last clause of this capitolo shows foresight on the part of the Gozitans. They petitioned to be allowed to import two hundred salmi of Sicilian grain, pleading that should a further Moorish invasion take place prior to the gathering of the harvest there would be famine among the population. The reply to this clause was as follows: taking into consideration the more pressing need of Sicily a promise could not then be given.

From the clauses of this capitolo we have a fair idea of conditions prevailing at that time in Gozo. Moorish invasion was a constant and very real fear and devastation was general in those invasions. A certain amount of nepotism and unfairness existed. The higher posts in the government were retained for favoured Sicilians, the king thereby keeping a sure hold of the island. It is evident from clause three that the people had a leaning towards hazardous games and the love of gambling was deep-rooted.

It is not out of place to mention here that the conditions prevailing in Malta and Gozo in the late Middle Ages were those common to all minor cities of the Kingdom of Sicily. In fact the capitoli of Caltagirone, Corleone, Girgenti, Lentini, Licata, and others of that period are more or less identical to those of Malta, and Gozo.

The first of this series of four capitoli is dated at Palermo, 4th May, 1438, I Indiction, and marked No. II. It is more or less a repetition of the petition made six years previously. The petitioners once more reminded the King of the hardships they were sustaining through the Moorish invasion of 1429. Using this plea the Gozitans petitioned for exemption from taxation and Excise Duty on goods exported to Gozo from Sicily. In this capitole the petitioners mention once more the aridity of the soil, their extreme poverty, and lack of means of support through the devastation caused by the Moorish invaders. These capitoli were submitted to the King and to the Vicreoy by Giovanni Vigiles, one of the Giurati of the island of Gozo.

This petition was granted on the same day as it was presented to the Viceroy. In a privilege attached to the petition was the permit granting all the requests of the Gozitans. It stated that the island Gozo was to receive as much grain as was needed from any port whatsoever free from Excise Duty; and in order to ensure that this was carried out the King gave orders that all Portulans, Viceportulans and all other minor portulans were to abide by these conditions.

The privilege states that the benefit of this condition was only to be enjoyed by the island of Gozo, and the inhabitants of that island were forbidden to trade with other places in the grain obtained tax-free from Sicily. As this excise-free merchandise was to be conveyed to Gozo on Gozitan vessels, the Viceroy obliged the masters of the vessels to furnish the necessary guarantees that the merchandise would be taken to Gozo and no other port (et perki nostra omnimoda intencioni e' ki li dicti habitaturi di Gozu haianu la dicta gracia, vi cumandamu expressamenti ki libere et sine contradicione aliqua ex sola tantum exibicione presentis permictiti li dicti Gaudisani cum quali si vogla navi oy navili et barki extrahiri di ciasquidunu di li dikti porti et carricaturi da undi vurrannu per portari in Gozu, comu e' dictu, per usu e provisioni di la dicta insola et non in altri loki, tucti quantitati di frumentu oy victuagli franki di omni dirittu di tracta,……..).

This concession to the island of Gozo in 1438 shows how the people of these islands were considered in no less a way than the inhabitants of the island of Sicily. Such concessions were granted on different occasions to the Sicilians of the Kingdom of Aragon. It also brings to our realization how great had been the disaster sustained by the Gozitans in the Moorish invasions of the first part of the 15th century and the hardships following the abduction of man-power and pillage of cattle.

On the 20th July, 1439, Notary Angelo de Manueli submitted another capitolo to the Viceroy of Sicily — marked No. III.

The Gozitans again, in this capitolo, draw attention to their woeful state of poverty which impeded their being able to nourish the soil to provide the crops necessary for their maintenance.

They drew attention to the petition, made in the previous year, through which they had been granted special privileges for the importation of grain and comestibles from Sicily. The Gozitans lamented that owing to loss of ships they had not been able to take advantage of the grant. The lack of vessels was due to the pillaging corsairs of Calabria. Once more the Gozitans drew attention to their penury which did not enable them to cultivate the land. Gozo was so close to the state of famine that they lacked of grain of corn or barley. They then stated that they had been spared from starvation on account of the generosity of Simone di Mazara and Antonio Mule who had sent, to Gozo, a supply of grain which saved them in their great extremity, (et si non per misser Simuni di Mazara et Antoni Mule, li quali mandaru in quista insola certi quantitati di frumentu, ja moriamu di fami).

Another clause in this capitolo complains of taxation enforced on the Gozitans. They mentioned how the Honourable Antonio Brunu had actually come to Gozo to collect twenty uncias in taxation. This had caused much surprise to the population of Gozo who were barely able to exist, let alone find the money levied. They pointed out how they thought that giving their service to the king to fight his enemies was surely sufficient, considering their extreme poverty and the aridity of their soil (la nostra paupertati, et grandi penuria supra quistu scoglu arridu). They ended by stating that so great was their poverty that had they had the means they would have left the island, and Gozo would have become deserted (fa la insola sirria disabitata).

The Giurati of Gozo concluded this capitolo by saying that they had come to an agreement with lu dictu Antoni Brunu regarding the taxation of the twenty uncias. He had consented to accept thirteen uncias at once, the balance to be paid in 18 days time. This sum of thirteen uncias had been collected from the whole island of Gozo and, to emphasize the strain incurred by the Gozitans to raise this sum, it was said that this money had been extracted from the very marrow of their bones (teste Deo, extrahirimu quasi di intra li ossa nostri). They begged that they be condoned the seven remaining uncias, taking into consideration their previous pleas of poverty and hunger and military service to the king.

The Viceroy granted this last petition in consideration of the conditions prevailing in Gozo.

The next capitolo — marked No. IV — dated at Palermo, 5th November, 1448, was submitted to the Viceroy by one of the Giurati of Gozo, named Cola de Algaria. This capitolo was on a matter of administrative procedure of the Consiglio Popolare. On the plea that the elected members of the Council were at times absent from the island of Gozo, conducting their personal affairs, it was inconvenient to postpone council meetings in which deliberations on important matters were to be taken, until their return. The permision was requested to hold council meetings when necessary even in the absence of certain memmbers. The council held under such conditions would consist of:- the Capitano della Verga, his Assessors, the Judges, the Giurati, and the four old Giurati (i.e., those elected for the previous session), and four worthy citizens of the island (et altri quatru boni homini di li princhipali di la terra).

This plea was granted by the Viceroy with the usual placet.

Another item of this capitolo refers to the procedure for election of the officials of the government. It was submitted that various, worthy citizens and their sons had placed themselves for election, but notwithstanding their excellent qualities and suitability, they had not been appointed. This had occurred because of the nomination of other persons less worthy should anyone form part of the Consiglio Popolare unless elected by popular vote and that those nominated de gracia should not be accepted.

Once again the Gozitans objected against payment of taxes on the usual plea of dire poverty and sterility of the soil. They stated that the levying of taxation is not a service to the king, but to the reverse, a disservice to the realm (by which we understand that the payment of taxes must have caused considerable unrest and resentment in Gozo against the ruling power). They now make reference to the manner in which the collector of taxes should perform his duty in the event of the taxation not being lifted. In such an event the collector would not collect the money from one or two citizens who had the reputation of being affluent: all Gozitans are poor, (perki tutti simu poviri), they pleaded, without exception and taxation should be borne equally by all citizens. Another request was that the collector of taxes should perform his duties personally, i.e., not by delegation.

It appears from the next item that certain privileges granted to Gozo by a previous Viceroy were not being respected, therefore they ask that the right granted to decide cases of minor importance be respected.

The last clause of this capitolo refers to another angle of the poverty of Gozo: the great lack or rather absence of wood for fuel on the island. From time immemorial the poor of Gozo had taken fallen twigs and branches, and gleaned the lands belonging to the crown. It now appears that the tenants of the said lands had forbidden the continuante of this age-old usage. On account of the duties performed by these poor people, duties which comprised turns of coast-watching and repairing of city walls (li dicti poviri su angariati a li guardii di la terra et a la maramma di li mura et multi altri angarii in serviciu di la regia maiestati), it was requested that they be granted permission to glean once more on the lands of the crown.

The last capitolo in this series — marked No. V — bears the date 14th May, 1453, I Indiction. It was submitted to the King at Naples, by Giovanni de Vigiles, Ambassador of the Università of Gozo.

His Majesty was informed of the capture of the two Moors (dui mori nigri) by the mounted coast-guard of the island. The Moors had been discovered on the shores and had told the guards that they were deserters from the Moorish ships, as it had been their desire to dwell in Gozo. The Gozitans well knew that their story was a fabrication and that they had been landed in Gozo with very ulterior motives. Therefore the two Moors were sold as slaves and the money obtained through this sale was used to purchase weapons to arm the poor of Gozo, to serve them for defence against invaders. As the money from this deal had been used in this manner, the King was beseeched to waive his rights for share of booty.

To this request the King gave his placet.

Once again the Gozitans ask that certain privileges granted to them be respected. It appears that a reprieve had been granted to criminals condemned by the local courts. Therefore the authority of the Gozo Courts were being held in contempt. They ask that cases of theft, whether of major or minor degree, should be brought before the court and persons found guilty of such crimes were to be punished accordingly.

The next item refers to the Jewish colony of Gozo. As the members of the colony had gradually shrugged of their duties of free service (li Judey di la dicta terra et insula si hagianu ysgravatu di multi angarii) which was normally performed by the Gozitans, they — the Jews — should be obliged to keep a horse for the defence of the Island in lieu of service.

The King consented to this measure with the stipulation that the horse should be kept solely for the use of the island in time of war, inclusive of a month before and one month after hostilities had ceased.

The last item of this capitolo refers to the appointment of the judge of Gozo. This office was of annual duration, the occupier being elected yearly. The judge was obliged before taking up his appointment, to present himself to the Viceroy of Sicily, from whom he obtained confirmation of his appointment. The Gozitans petitioned in this capitolo that this procedure be abandoned, as the sea journey to Sicily incurred considerable peril. Besides during the absence of the judge, the population suffered through the lack of administration of justice. It appears that the judge at this time, whose name was Notary Andrea di Bongeminu, was the only legal man in Gozo and he had held the appointment of judge for many terms. He was a Gozitian by birth, he spoke the language of the people, and, to quote the words of the capitolo: "knew everyone on the island high and low" (li dictu notaru Andria esti oriundu di la dicta insula sa et intendi la lingua et canuxi lu pichulu et lu grandi et [p.71] sa li constumi, consuetudini et usanczi di la dicta terra et insula). He was also loved by his fellow countrymen and held in great esteem and trust.

The Gozitans petitioned the King to appoint permanently Bongeminu as a judge, taking into consideration his knowledge of the local language, his excellent qualities and capabilities (maxime per ki lu dictu notaru Andria sa et intendi la lingua di ka dicta insula et esti aptu racione lingue alu dictu officiu). It was furthur pleaded that this appointment should be made in spite of all precedents to the contrary, and that the matter be treated with urgency.

King Alfonso graciously added his placet to this petition and Gozo had her permanent judge as desired.

In conclusion we notice time after time the plea for relief of taxation in Gozo on account of the sterility and poorness of the soil. It is hard for us who know Gozo today to picture a state of aridity in a land so fertile and flourishing in agriculture. We can only assume that the continuous Moorish incursions caused the agricultural population to desert their holding through fear. It is also likely that the invaders burned crops and uprooted trees, and possibly robbed the island of cattle. This last would contribute considerably to the poorness of the soil.

It is to be noted that many of the surnames of Gozitan families mentioned in these capitoli, such as: Gallo, de Manueli, Mazara, Mula, de Algaria, di Bongeminu, were already extinct in the 18th century. We find this fact mentioned in the manuscript work on Gozo by Canon Gian Pietro Agius de Soldanis, entitled: GOZO ANTICO E MODERNO, SACRO E PROFANO.

We notice also that the last capitolo, approved by King Alfonso, is signed at Naples, at Castel Nuovo, and bears the date 1458. The reason for the change from Palermo to Naples is obvious. King Alfonso, surnamed "the Magnanimous," having liberated Naples from Angevin rule, entered that city on the 12th June, 1442, and was recognised King of Naples by Pope Eugen IV in 1443. Alfonso assumed the title of "Re delle due Sicilie" which title then appeared for the first time on coins bearing the words: Siciliae citra et ultra. With the creation of the new kingdom Naples became the capital: Palermo was no longer the centre of the Royal Courts and Sicily became of lesser importance than erstwhile: it was a diminutio capitis. Reading through the capitoli of twenty-one years from 1482 to 1458, we cannot but be impressed by the dire state of Gozo through piracy of her ships on the high seas and Moorish incursions on land. Likewise we cannot but be impressed by the unfailing courage and spirit of the Gozitans in spite of great odds. They were determined to maintain their privileges and government of the island. It is also shown from these capitoli that the King and Viceroy readily granted their demands, which acquiescence was most likely due to admiration of the courage and endurance of so small an island. The two Moorish spies referred in capitolo No. V. who tried to pose as deserters could not deceive the Gozitans of the 15th century. As today the Gozitans were gifted with a subtle strain of astuteness which made them masters of most situations.

Gozo

Gozo's fascinating history is closely intertwined with the story of its sister Island of Malta. Gozo shares the colourful legacy of the many different peoples who have invaded, traded and settled in the Maltese Islands over the last seven thousand years.

Human habitation here dates back to around 5000 B.C.- and the oldest known settements are in Gozo. The earliest settlers came from Sicily, some 88 kilometres to the North, so they would have reached Gozo before Malta. As early as 3600BC, the people of Gozo were builidng sophisitcated stone structures, including the Ġgantija Temples, now some of the oldest freestanding stone buildings in the world. Their remains, with UNESCO World Heritage status, can still be seen in ix-Xagħra.

The historical record begins with the Phoenicians, the famous Mediterranean traders, from today's Lebanon, who introduced cloth dyeing and maritime trade to Malta. Their close relatives, the Carthaginians, succeeded them and, after a brief period of Greek influence and the three Punic Wars, Gozo and Malta became part of the Roman Empire. The Romans introduced the code of law and used the Maltese Islands as a hub for honey and olive oil exports. They left behind villas with lavish mosaic floors and a maze of late-Roman catacombs.

Christianity was brought to Malta in 60 A.D. by St. Paul, and properly took hold under the Byzantines, from the Eastern Roman Empire. In the late 9th Century A.D. the Arabs, after taking Sicily, took control of the Maltese Islands. They introduced the Water Mill and the cotton plant that proved to be the mainstay of the islands' economy for centuries to come. The Arabsinfluenced our present language, gave us the names of Malta and Għawdex (Maltese for Gozo), together with the oldest village and family names on the islands.

The Normans re-established Christianity in Malta and Gozo in 1090. There followed a period when the Maltese islands were handed around the aristocracies of Germany, France and Spain. The islands were taken over in turn by the Swabians (1194); the Angevins (1268); the Aragonese (1283) and finally, the Castilians (1410). Malta and Gozo together were often leased in fiefdoms under the feudal system then practised throughout Europe. There are few records about this feudal period, but in Gozo, the Angevins had a cemetery in today's ir-Rabat , where French nobles and crusader casualties were almost certainly buried. Several tombstones and artefacts from the period were saved from destruction and can still be found in the Museum of Archaeology in ir-Rabat (Victoria).

The crucial period of the Hospitaller Knights of the Military Order of St. John – now commonly known as the Knights of Malta– commenced in 1530, after they lost their base in Rhodes to the Ottoman Turks. The Knights ruled Malta until the arrival of Napoleon in 1798. At first, the new rulers still yearned to recapture Rhodes and as a result, did not adequately improve the islands' defences leaving them open to ever more ferocious attacks by Turkish corsairs. Gozo, in particular, suffered terribly.

In 1551 a strong Turkish naval force attempted an invasion of Malta. It was rebuffed and, rather than leave empty handed, the Turks attacked the less well protected island of Gozo, laying siege to the Citadel at the centre of the capital. With its medieval walls crumbling under constant cannon fire, the Citadel withstood assault after assault until, with all hope of help from Malta lost, the defenders begged for an honourable capitulation. Tragically for the population (then numbering around 5000) the surrender terms were far from honourable: excepting only 40 of the elderly and infirm, Gozo's entire population was chained and taken into slavery.

The Turkish raids culminated in the Great Siege of Malta in 1565. The Knights of St John and the Maltese won a narrow victory which reduced the Ottoman enthusiasm for attacks on the Maltese Islands and led to the Order of St. John establishing itself permanently in Malta. The result was the building of a new fortified capital city – Valletta, and – eventually – the strengthening of fortifications in Gozo too.

The next 230 years were a time of relative prosperity. The population expanded, villages became towns, areas of coast were settled or re-inhabited and Baroque architecture sprang up across the islands. This is the period that created many of today's Maltese icons, from churches to the massive fortifications.

The rule of the Knights came to an abrupt end in June 1798 when Napoleon captured the Maltese Islands with unexpected ease. The Grand Master capitulated after a feeble, sporadic and confused resistance. Napoleon made his grand entry into Valletta and within a week Grandmaster Von Hompesch, accompanied by a few knights, left the Island unceremoniously. Malta became part of Republican France with its new revolutionary ideals. In his short stay in Malta, Napoleon abolished the nobility, revised the civil laws, and introduced education for all classes. He also launched the judicial system of trial by jury, something unthinkable in the royal courts that still ruled most of Europe.

The French, in dire need of gold to pay the army started to strip palaces, Auberges and other buildings of everything of value – not a practise likely to endear them to the local population. The French Governor, conveniently forgetting previous promises, next turned his attention to the churches. Feeling among the highly religious population was already running high and the looting of their churches was the last straw. A mere three months after their arrival on the islands the French were in trouble.

Gozo was the first to overthrow the French occupiers. Under the leadership the Archpriest Saverio Cassar, they revolted and surrounded the French in the Citadel and in Fort Chambrai (above Mġarr harbour). A small number of British troops landed on Gozo shortly after this and the French surrendered to them in October 1798. On Malta, the French garrison locked itself up in Valletta for two years, but here too they eventually fell to the Maltese with British support.

Under the Treaty of Paris (1814) Malta was confirmed as a British Possession. As steam replaced sail, Malta became an important coaling station, all the more so after the opening of the Suez Canal in 1869. The ever present problem of the water supply also received urgent attention. In Gozo an aqueduct system was constructed to bring fresh water to ir-Rabat (Victoria). Part of this aqueduct still stands today, crossing the main road from the West of the island into the capital. Another British construction that remains operational is the Ta' Ġurdan Lighthouse, sitting proudly on a hill above the village of l-Għasri.

It was during the British period that Gozo became a separate diocese from that of Malta. The Gozitans had been petitioning the Pope since 1798 to grant them an independent diocese. Finally, On 9 June 1855, three representatives of the Gozitans brought up the matter in a private audience with Pope Pius IX. The kind Pontiff pitied the petitioners and promised his support. However, it was not until 16 September 1864 that Pope Pius IX, through the Papal Bull Singulari Amore (With remarkable love), allowed the islands of Gozo and Comino to secede from the diocese of Malta. On 22 September 1864, Bishop Buttigieg was elected the first bishop of Gozo and on October 23 he made his solemn entry into the Cathedral Church of Santa Marija in Gozo's Citadel.

The military importance of Malta and its islands was clearly demonstrated during the Crimean War (1854-56) and the First World War (1914-18) when Malta became a rear base for the departure of troops and a receiving station for casualties. But it was in the Second World War (1939-45), that Malta was brought into the frontline of operations and played a crucial strategic role. Gozo lacked targets of military importance and fared much better than the main island, which was continuously targeted by Axis air-raids and was nearly subdued by hunger and deprivation. It was saved by the Santa Marija Convoy which arrived just in time on 15th August 1942. A few months earlier, on April 15th King George VI had awarded the George Cross Medal for gallantry to the entire population of the Island Fortress of Malta.

After the destruction of the war, the Maltese Islands started to rebuild themselves; political parties emerged and yearned for Independence. Meanwhile, the British Empire was slowly transforming into a Commonwealth of Nations and Malta was losing its strategic military importance. Malta officially asked the British Government for independence in 1962 and after tough negotiations, this was granted on 21st September 1964.

Malta never looked back. It became a Republic in 1974 and on 31st March 1979, the last of the British military personnel sailed out of Grand Harbour on what is today known as Freedom Day. Finally, following a popular referendum, on May 1st 2004, Malta joined the European Union.

Travel and Tourism

The Sister Isles

Gozo & Comino
Some beautiful treasures are waiting to be discovered...Discover Gozo

Find out about the Sister Islands of Gozo and Comino, about how easy it is getting there and getting around, about the choice of accommodation available - from top-range hotels to idyllic farmhouses. read about what to see and do, check out useful information about services and contacts to help you plan your trip.

Whether you decide to spend your entire stay on Gozo or Comino, or if you want to make it a side-trip during your holiday in Malta, you will find that these are truly special places.

Steeped in myth, Gozo is thought to be the legendary Calypso's isle of Homer's Odyssey - a peaceful, mystical backwater. Baroque churches and old stone farmhouses dot the countryside. Gozo's rugged landscape and spectacular coastline await exploration with some of the Mediterranean's best dive sites.

The island also comes complete with historical sites, forts and amazing panoramas, as well as one of the archipelago's best-preserved prehistoric temples, Ġgantija.

To discover the true magic of swimming, diving and enjoying all the activities the sea has to offer, Comino is the Island that must be explored. The island's Blue Lagoon, with its safe bathing in bright turquoise waters, makes a memorable day out by boat.

The island is tiny in size, with just one hotel, but it is otherwise uninhabited and is surrounded by the most scintillating and transparent waters in the Mediterranean. A natural swimming pool, many snorkel, scuba dive and anchor their yachts for a day of swimming and relaxing. In winter, Comino is great for walkers and photographers. Without urban areas or cars, there is no pollution or noise - just quiet and serenity

What to See and Do

In today's stressful lifestyle, taking time to unwind and just be has become an absolute necessity. For those who wish to switch off and regenerate, Gozo is the place to be.

Historically, the island has always been distinct from mainland Malta; different milestones, traditions, happenings and topography have distinguished the island both on a national scale and as a travel destination. A lower population density and the slower process of urbanisation have contributed to conserving the island's characteristic aura, which wins over the traveller who is looking to slow down.

Wherever you look, the sea is never more than a stone's throw away and it's Gozo's remarkable coastline that stimulates the imagination so strongly: tiny creeks, beaches of red sand, turquoise bays, stretches of limestone criss-crossed with tiny saltpans and majestic high cliffs falling in a sheer drop into the clear waters.

Food and drink are a big part of daily life in Gozo. A hilly, fertile Island surrounded by the Mediterranean, it is in an excellent location for healthy and tasty produce. There is a wide variety of restaurants that offer both fine dining as well as more casual eateries offering traditional food. Gozo is host to some of the best award-winning restaurants on the islands and with picturesque views of harbours and bays, it's easy to find a restaurant in a spectacular setting. Restaurants abound in Rabat, Mġarr and in the fishing villages of Marsalforn and Xlendi.

Off-the-beaten track, you will find small local producers offering tours and hands-on experiences, including fruit-picking, olive oil and wine tasting.

Village bars open early in the morning for the early risers who attend the first mass of the day and close fairly late at night, catering to the socialising needs of locals and visitors.

- ✓ Archaeological Sites
- ✓ Beaches & Bays
- ✓ Church & Religious Sites
- ✓ Cinemas
- ✓ Dive Sites -Boat
- ✓ Dive Sites- Shore
- ✓ Diving Centres
- ✓ Entertainment Venues
- ✓ Fortifications & Towers

- ✓ Gardens
- ✓ Language Schools
- ✓ Museums & Galleries
- ✓ Natural Attractions
- ✓ Other Attractions
- ✓ Parks & Gardens
- ✓ Shopping
- ✓ Sports Facilities
- ✓ Sports Service Providers
- ✓ Theatre & Opera
- ✓ Towns & Villages
- ✓ Visitor Attractions
- ✓ Wedding Venues
- ✓ Restaurants - 1st Class
- ✓ Restaurants - 2nd Class
- ✓ Restaurants - 3rd Class
- ✓ Vineyards

Archaeological Sites

Ġgantija Temples

Ġgantija Temples are one of the most important archaeological sites in the world and date from around 3600 to 3200 BC.

Due to the gigantic dimensions of the megaliths, locals believed that the temples were the work of giants. This particular temple site in Gozo bears witness to this ancient legend: its name, Ġgantija, is Maltese for giant.

The Ġgantija megalithic complex consists of two temples surrounded by a massive common boundary wall, which was built using the alternating header and stretcher technique, with some of the megaliths exceeding five metres in length and weighing over fifty tons.

Built with rough, coralline limestone blocks, each temple contains five apses connected by a central corridor leading to the innermost trefoil section.

Xagħra Stone Circle

The Xagħra Stone Circle is an underground funerary complex, situated in Xagħra on the Maltese island of Gozo. It was first discovered by John Otto Bayer in the 1820s and rediscovered in 1964 after Gozitan researcher Joe Attard Tabone examined a painting by Charles Brochtorff in the National Library in Valletta.

The site was excavated by a joint team from the University of Malta, the Maltese Museums Department and the University of Cambridge. The excavation uncovered the burial ground of the same community which practiced its rituals in the nearby Ggantija Temples, dating principally to the period from 3000 to 2500 BC.

The most notable discoveries include more than 200,000 human bones and prehistoric art relating to the builders of the prehistoric Maltese temples.

An earlier chambered tomb on site dates to the period between 4100 and 3800 BC.

Beaches & Bays

Dahlet Qorrot
This is a tiny picturesque fishing cove and a tranquil, isolated spot on the north-east coast below Nadur and Qala. The bay is a popular local beauty spot. The craggy coastline and clear waters are perfect for snorkelling. The bay is still used by local fishermen: a few boathouses line the shore. The ledges and small caves double up as shade areas. There is a snack-bar facility in the summer only. In winter, you will find the bay the perfect spot to sit and read, watch the waves and enjoy solitude

Dwejra Bay

Dwejra is perhaps the archipelago's most spectacular natural landmark. Here, geology, time and sea have worked together to produce some of the most remarkable scenery on the Islands - the Inland Sea, Fungus Rock, sheer cliffs and a rocky coastline.

Apart from the topography visible above sea and ground, there are also some fascinating underwater caves which provide excellent dive sites. The Inland Sea, and Dwejra Bay itself, were created millions of years ago when two limestone caves collapsed. The shallow inland lagoon is linked to the sea via a 50-metre cave. The `Sea' is used by fishermen, swimmers and as access point for divers. Overlooking the lagoon is the Chapel of St. Anne, built in 1963 on the site of a much older church. The other natural landmark here is the legendary Fungus Rock.

Hondoq Ir-Rummien

On the coast below the village of Qala lies Ħondoq ir-Rummien, a small cove which is popular with snorkellers because of its deep and clear water and the small caves at water level.

Access to the sea is from bathing ladders. The cove has good views over Comino. The coastline nearby is dotted with traditional salt pans, some of which are still actively used to `harvest' salt throughout the summer months.

Marsalforn

Marsalforn, meaning 'bakery harbour', is Gozo's main seaside town. During the summer, it becomes a bustling, lively resort. There is a small but pleasant sandy bank on the harbour with safe bathing and good rocky coastline towards Qbajjar which is excellent for snorkelling.

The resort has a good range of accommodation from seafront self-catering apartments to hotels. Marsalforn is characterised by its harbour-side cafes and restaurants, many serving fresh fish. The small harbour is the main port for a fleet of traditional 'luzzijiet' trawlers and smaller fishing boats. The beauty of Marsalforn is its relaxed atmosphere, even in the height of summer.

Ramla Bay

Ramla is Gozo's largest sandy bay and one of the most beautiful on the Maltese Islands. The beach here is of a deep, reddish-gold hue. The bay is surrounded by countryside and nestles below steep terraced hills and the mythical Calypso's Cave.

There are no hotels or tourist developments nearby, but the beach side has several snack bars and cafes. The beach has its own landmark - a white statue of the Virgin Mary. Ramla is a superb spot to while away the hours - even in peak summer months, there always seems to be space on beach. In winter, you can find yourself alone. The area is excellent walking country. Swimming here is safe and the waters are clear and clean. There are some smooth, underwater boulders a few metres out in the central strip, but these are easily negotiated. On windy days, white surf rolling on the sand is an added attraction and fun for young bathers. The best approach to the bay is from Nadur or Xagħra, down a bamboo-lined valley. The road from Marsalforn, via Calypso's Cave, is rather steep and rough though it is passable by car.

Of historical interest in the bay are some Roman ruins burried under the sand near the present-day cafes, and a 'fougasse' - a kind of primative mortar developed by the Knights which was fired from a rock-cut shaft to defend the bay during the 18th century.Beach management at Ramla Bay is operated by GAIA Foundation and includes the services of lifeguards

Wied Il-Ghasri

Wied il-Għasri is very popular with divers who like to explore the surrounding underwater caves. The very narrow bay is a haven for those who seek a quiet bathing area.

Wied il-Għasri has its source at Dbieġi Hill. It winds its way through Għasri between Żebbuġ and Ġordan Hill and flows into the sea between very high impressive cliffs. A very interesting spot in this place is a cave close to the shore in which a shaft was hewn up to the top of the steep cliffs. A mill made up of several pails used to be rigged up in order to bring up the sea water to fill the neighbouring saltpans.

Xlendi Bay

The delightful sea inlet, known as Xlendi Bay, lies at the end of a deep, lush ravine which was once a river bed.

Until the mid-20th century, Xlendi was a small fishing port and a restful summer resort for a few locals and Maltese. The bay is now on the must-visit list of most day-trippers to the Island, but it is worthwhile lingering a night or two to enjoy the sunsets. The bay still retains a peaceful atmosphere and is surprisingly undeveloped though there is a good choice of accommodation from apartments to hotels; most options have sea views. Xlendi is flanked by steep cliff. For some of the best views, climb the stairs up the cliffs to the right. Bathing in Xlendi is usually off the rocks along the bay with access down ladder into the deep crystal clear water. On the left side of the bay, two tiers of pathways provide ample space for both a walkway and a flat space to spread out a towel and sunbathe.

On the promontory is Xlendi Tower, built in 1650. It commands superb sea views and stand on a scenic coastline pitted with hand-dug salt pans.

Churches & Religious Sites
Church of St. Gregory The Great

The parish church of Ta' Kerċem is the only church in Gozo which is jointly dedicated to two saints - St Gregory and Our Lady of Perpetual Help.

The village originally grew around a chapel dedicated to Pope St. Gregory the Great, built around 1581. The site gained prominance due to the annual traditional St. Gregory procession from the Mother Church in ir-Rabat (Victoria) to this chapel, on the saint's feast, 12th March. The chapel was however replaced by the present parish church in 1851 and this was in turn enlarged in 1906-10. Ta' Kerċem became a distinct parish in 1885 and later the same the same year, the church was co-dedicated to Our Lady of Perpetual Help.

With two patron saints, the village has two festas, that of St Gregory in March and the (nowadays rather larger) feast of Our Lady of Perpetual Help on the second Sunday of July.

Church of The Sacred Heart

Il-Fontana, these days a suburb of ir-Rabat (Victoria), lies on the road to ix-Xlendi and traditionally most of the fishermen who operated out of ix-Xlendi Bay lived in this village. In the late nineteenth century they started to collect money in order to build a church. The foundation stone of the present church, dedicated to the Sacred Heart of Jesus, was laid on 29th January 1892. It was consecrated exactly thirteen years later on 29th January 1905. Il-Fontana was established as a parish in 1911 and the spectacular village festa is celebrated each year in 2nd or 3rd week of June

Nativity Of Our Lady Church

The parish church of ix-Xagħra is dedicated to the Nativity of the Virgin Mary, locally known as 'Il-Bambina', and the fine marble interior of this church contains a particularly beautiful marble statue of the young virgin Mary 'Il-Bambina'. This marble statue brought to Gozo from Marseilles in 1878.

The church is also referred to as il-Vittorja (Our Lady of Victories) as its feast day, which is celebrated on 8th September, also commemorates the victory of the Knights of Malta over the Turks in the Great Siege of 1565.

The parish of ix-Xagħra was established early, by Bishop David Cocco-Palmieri in 1688 with the original seat being the chapel of Saint Antony Abbot which still stands in the village.

The present church, like many others, grew from an older building first recorded late in the seventeenth century. The foundation stone of the church we see today was laid in 1815 and the church was consecrated in 1878. The fourth Collegiate of Gozo was established at ix-Xagħra in 1900 and the title of Basilica was conferred on the parish in 1967

Our Lady Of Loreto Church

Għajnsielem became an autonomous parish by Papal decree in 1855. The Old Parish Church still stands but as the population of the village grew, a larger church was needed. Works on a new church in Gothic-Lombard style and in the shape of a Latin cross begun in 1924.

Work on the building was intermittent. Work was halted by World War One and two accidents in which the master mason Toni Vella broke his legs falling from the building. The first architect resigned, the second died and in all the church had four overseeing architects.

The church we see today was finally completed with the blessing of the bell tower in June 1979.

The church is dedicated to Our Lady of Loreto and when the new Church was finished, the titular statue was transferred from the Old Church to the new one. The fine statue was made by Gallard et Fils of Marseilles and arrived in Gozo on 14th October 1866 to be carried in procession from Mġarr Harbour to Għajnsielem

St. George's Basilica

The parish originated in medieval times (definitely before 1450) and the foundation stone of the present church was laid in 1672. It is rightly referred to as the marble basilica, as it is entirely covered with marble.

The bronze and gold gilded canopy over the high altar is indeed impressive, but the main attraction is a statue of the patron saint,

St. George, sculpted in wood by Pawlu Azzopardi in 1838. It is the first titular statue acquired by a parish church in Gozo.

All paintings in the dome and ceiling are by Giovanni Battista Conti of Rome. Mattia Preti, Giuseppe Cali, Michele Busuttil, Giuseppe Fenech, Francesco Zahra, Fortunato Venuti, Injazju Cortis, Ramiro Cali', Filippo Cosimo, Giuseppe D'Arena, Salvatore Bondi', Roberto Dingli and Stefano Erardi are other famous artists.

The liturgical feast of St. George Martyr falls on April 23rd.

St. Joseph Church

The parish church of il-Qala was designed by Dun Ġużepp Diacono, the same architect-priest who designed the church of l-Għasri. It was constructed between 1882 and 1889, when he was serving as parish priest in il-Qala. The church is baroque in style, like many of Gozo's churches (whether they were built in the seventeenth century or the twentieth!).

Il-Qala became a parish on 3rd February 1872, the first to be established after the creation of the Diocese of Gozo (separate from Malta). The seat of the parish church was the church of the Immaculate Conception of Our Lady until St Joseph's was completed in 1889. The church was consecrated in 1904 and became Archipresbyteral in 1965.

The annual village festa is celebrated in early August.

St. Margaret Church

Ta' Sannat was one of the first villages in Gozo to become a parish separate from ir-Rabat in 1688. The building of the present parish church dedicated to St Margaret the Martyr commenced on the site of a smaller church in 1718, but underwent several structural changes in the 1860s.

The church was first consecrated in 1755 and then, after structural adaptations, it was re-consecrated in 1868. It was raised to Archipresbyteral status in 1893. The altarpiece was painted by the well-known local artist Stefano Erardi.

The festa is celebrated each year around the third week of July.

St. Mary Church

The church of St. Mary in Żebbuġ is spectacular for its onyx (Gozo alabaster) interior - a recent addition to a much older church.

There is believed to have been a church on the hill of iż-Żebbuġ since time immemorial. A chapel dedicated to the Assumption of

Our Lady is first recorded in 1615 - and noted by the Bishop of the time, paying a pastoral visit, to be one of the best kept chapels on the island.

Around 1640, the community in iż-Żebbuġ felt the need to build a new larger chapel, which was finished by 1644 and the village gained parish status in 1688. The chapel once again proved too small, and the people began to build another much larger church on the site in 1690 which was consecrated in 1726. This was the first church after Gozo Cathedral to be built with aisles.

Today the church is richly embellished with Gozo onyx. This onyx, sometimes referred to as Gozo alabaster, was unearthed in a field in the vicinity of the church, and is the village's pride and joy. The church's altar, pulpit, font, chandeliers, and confessionals are all now of carved onyx, transforming the parish church into an extravagant and unique attraction.

St. Paul's Church

The church in Marsalforn is dedicated to Saint Paul Shipwrecked. As recorded in the Acts of the Apostles, St.Paul was shipwrecked on Malta, but according to tradition it was from Marsalforn that he subsequently embarked for Sicily and Rome.

The church was originally raised in the fourteenth century but has been rebuilt and enlarged many times. The foundation stone of the present church was laid in 1730.

The feast of St Paul is celebrated on 10th February.

Boat Diving
Billinghurst Cave
Billingshurst Cave is found to the west of Reqqa Point in the Northern part of Gozo. The top of the cave entrance is just above the surface and the bottom is at 27 meters. A long tunnel called The Railway Tunnel, leads to another cave deep inside the rock where divers can surface. Entry is from Reqqa Point. Immediately inside the cave there are plenty of red sponges, soft corals, cardinalfish and other types of marine life. On the way back, the sight of the blue open water with the sun shining through from the outer reef, is breathtaking and perfect for silhouette photographs.

Dwejra Point
Dwejra is one of the most spectacular dive sites in Malta, with deep water (60 metres) and many caves and arches. The most dramatic is the 35 metre long tunnel that opens from the Inland Sea to the open sea, where the bottom drops suddenly. The clear waters and

depths can be deceptive. This dive is the right place for divers looking for the abundant marine life

Fessej Rock

This dive site is found offshore from the Mgarr ix-Xini inlet along the south shore near Mgarr Harbour. Fessej Rock is a tall, circular and vertical column of rock which rises about 15 metres (50 feet) above the water and plunges vertically 50 metres (165 feet) to the seabed, amidst a number of huge boulders. The average depth of the dive is of 30 metres (100 feet), and one encounters large schools of fish, tube worms and squat lobsters, dentex and amberjacks. Barracuda, tuna and grouper, as well as octopus and other lobster can be found on this dive.....

Fungus Rock

Fungus Rock is a huge rock in Dwejra Bay, on the western coast of Gozo. Access is only by boat. The average depth is of 40 metres. This isolated rock has a hole running through its northern part. Underwater, the scenery is as impressive as above, with vertical walls, fissures, gulleys and caverns created by boulders, which provide excellent habitat for the largest groupers. Looking upwards, one can often see tuna, amberjacks and barracudas. The walls of the rock are covered in algae, sea urchins, tube worms, starfish, bristle worms and sea potatoes, with their brilliant red colour.

San Dimitri Point

San Dimitri Point is at the most westerly point in Gozo. It is an imposing rock jutting out from the shore, and is only accessible by boat. The first part of the dive is quite gentle, after which one comes across a large boulder with smaller ones littering the seabed at a depth of about 30 metres. Throughout the dive one can come across large shoals of barracuda. Grouper, dentex and damselfish are also commonly seen, as well as octopus and moray eels.

Shore Diving

Crocodile Rock & Coral Cave

The crocodile-shaped rock is just offshore between Dwejra Point and Fungus rock. It can be reached both by boat or from the rocky shore. Heading westerly towards the left of the rock, one finds a square shute pointing towards the deeper water, revealing a steep cliff. The cliff drops vertically down to 38 metres, where the seabed is covered in boulders. In this area one can see groupers and shoals of salema. Keeping the cliff-face to the right, one will eventually reach the Coral Cave. This is a huge semi-circular opening with 20 metres across the sandy bottom, at a depth of around 22 metres.

Within the cave, using a torch, one can see different types of coral sponges, virgin lace, and the quite rare marine goldfish.

Double Arch Reef

This dive site is found a short distance to the east of Xwieni Bay, on the north coast of Gozo. It requires a 200 metre swim in a northerly direction, where a drop-off is reached. Nearby there are two distinctive holes through a vertical rock face, which are known as Double Arch Reef. The top of the rock is at a depth of 16 metres, whilst the rest goes down to a depth of 36 metres, with the lower arch being the larger of the two holes. On the way one encounters seagrass inhabited by cuttlefish, octopus and even the seahorse. Often a large shoal of of small barracuda can be seen in this area.

Ghasri Valley

This dive site is located between Reqqa Point and Forna Point, on the North coast of Gozo. Ghasri Valley is a spectacular deep cut which widens as it reaches the sea. This dive site is also known as the Blue Dome or Cathedral Cave. This dive is ideal for all levels of divers. It commences on a shingle beach where the water is shallow, but becomes deeper at a maximum depth of 30 metres. The seabed is covered in anemones, and large boulders covered in algae, sea urchins and starfish. One can also sea damselfish, seabreams, and scorpionfish, and might even come across a seahorse. The cave itself is only 5 metres below surface and leads through a domed vault, where one can surface and breathe freely. The seabed of the cave is covered in boulders, but the most impressive part is the view to the outside ocean. Towards the end of the valley, at a depth of approximitely 20 metres, one can encounter octopus and groupers.

Il-Kantra:

This site is located inside the western entrance to an inlet called Mġarr ix-Xini. At the western side of the inlet a number of rare fish can be seen, such as the flying gurnard, the red gurnard, the stargazer and if luck the John Dory. Other species include seabream, scorpionfish, small octopus and large cuttlefish. There are also two caves. On entering the caves one can see anemones and even some shrimps hidden amongst the walls. The seabed away from the cliff face is of coarse sand, with occasional seagrass, above which rarer fish are found.

Mġarr Ix-Xinia

The caverns at 10m and 16m in this bay can be reached from both Mġarr ix-Xini and Ta' Ċenċ. The cliff continues underwater to a depth of 30 metres where it gives way to large boulders. These provide ample hiding places for groupers. This dive site is very popular with photographers due to a variety of species of fish, from gurnard, stargazers and even seahorses. There is also a cave, inside which one can surface.

Reqqa Point
This is the northernmost tip of Gozo. The beach road is rough, the entry is tricky with a strong swell, but it is a fantastic dive. The reef consists of a parapet at a depth of 30 metres and then a drop to 60 metres. However, there is an excellent vantage point at 15 metres. Here one is literally in a cloud of small fish feeding on the nutrient-rich waters. Large shoals of dentex have feeding frenzies, groupers are large and plentiful. Adding to this, there are large caves and deep water.

The Blue Hole & The Chimney
This site is located at the bottom of Dwejra Point. It is a shore dive, which is reached via a fairly difficult walk over rough coralline limestone, however steps have been carved into the rocks leading down to the Blue Hole. This is a natural rock formation carved out over the centuries by wind and waves which goes down to a depth of 26 metres. The hole is about one metre above sea level and and no more than 10 metres wide and 5 metres across. However, a few

metres down, this gives way to unlimited access to the sea on exiting a huge archway. A large cave can also be found at the bottom of the hole. The Chimney is entered one diver at a time through a fissure in the almost vertical rock. This opens up at a depth of around 8 metres. Througout the dive, one can see various species of fish, starfish and bristle worms. This dive is perfect for photography.

Xlendi Cave

Xlendi Cave is found in Xlendi Bay. It is best to swim across the bay either on the surface on underwater. The maximum depth of this dive is 12 metres. The cave is a bent tunnel leading from one side to another of the rock wall. At the entrance of the cave floor one can see goatfish, damselfish and cardinalfish. The cave walls are brightly coloured with starfish, sponges, algae and bristle worms. Further on in the tunnel there are large boulders and it gets progressively shallower. Towards the end of the tunnel, the seabed is covered with smooth rocks and shingle.

Xlendi Reef

Xlendi Reef is located in the middle of Xlendi Bay. Part of the reef forms a pinnacle, which reaches up to within a metre of the surface. The reef is covered with seaweed and small fish. One can also see large numbers of damselfish, small groups of grey mullets as well as various species of wrasses and seabreams. The base of the reef is littered with large boulders. The reef comes to an end below the steep cliffs.

Diving Centres

Atlantis Diving

Atlantis Diving Centre was first established in 1993 and has been a family run business throughout. In the early days it was part of the Atlantis Hotel, which was demolished in 2010 to make way for a development of luxury apartments. Our current premises, just across the road from our previous dive centre, are brand new and occupy a large area on the ground floor and basement of that development.

We have always strived to achieve the highest standards throughout our business, whether it is organising your special holiday or replacing your broken fin strap. Of course, we do our utmost to make sure you enjoy your diving to the full. We are one of only two dive centres on the Maltese Islands with full EUF accreditation. We also believe we are one of the friendliest dive centres but only our customers can provide accreditation for that.

A large percentage of our customers return each year, (several even make two or three visits per year) and many have been coming since the late 1990s.

Our team of fully qualified instructors can provide you with any additional training you desire from basic courses to technical mixed-gas diving.

Some members of our team have been with us for several years and have intimate knowledge of those special dive sites, where to find those rare elusive fish or that secret little cave or niche. Whether you prefer deep or shallow, caverns or caves, boat or shore, wreck or scenic, day or night dives we can arrange it.

Blue Waters Dive Cove

We are a Gozo diving centre certified by PADI and by BSAC and fully licenced by the Malta Tourism Authority. We are a team of young yet experienced instructors, our rental equipment is brand new and the training facilities are excellent.

We are situated in the village of Qala just on top of the harbour. Our village has kept the true character of Gozo: quite and quaint with a very laid-back feeling. In our village we have excellent restaurants serving a big variety of local food, favourite international dishes and also oriental cuisine. There is also a choice of bars to enjoy your favourite tipple or a nice coffee whilst enjoying the most awesome views of the channel. Other facilities such as pharmacy, a number of grocer stores and a stationery ensure that you will find anything you need just 5 minutes walk away.

With us you will enjoy the true character of Gozo while having the opportunity to dive all the different diving sites around the island. All the dive sites are not more than a 20 minute drive from our village.

The dedication and friendly character of our instructors will guarantee good dive fun while knowing that your safety is always the top priority. We offer various dive packages, training courses, accompanied diving, boat dives and night dives.

We also offer complete holiday services such as car hire, accommodation and return airport transfers.

Our instructors and crew are fluent in English, Italian and German and will ensure that you get the most both while bubbling away under water or on terra firma.

Bubbles Dive Centre

We're an official PADI 5 star Dive Resort and offer the complete range of diving activities, whether you are a complete beginner, want to improve your diving skills and experience, make diving your career and become a professional or just want to experience the wonderful underwater world in Gozo.

We Care and we are very different. From the moment you arrive here you'll be greeted in a warm and friendly manner, your individual needs will be discussed and we'll put together a programme of diving that suits you. We only dive in small groups maximum 4 people per instructor / guide.

We Care about the environment and for every diving certification made we donate a proportion of our profit to Project AWARE and we actively participate in marine conservation projects and we are very proud to have won 3rd prize in Project AWARE's global Dive Against Debris campaign.

Calypso Diving Centre

Spectacular Diving in Gozo's azure waters! Operating since 1985, we are one of the longest established dive centre on the island of Gozo. Calypso Diving Centre is a PADI Dive Centre and BSAC Centre of Excellence, operating from modern, superbly located facilities on the seafront in Marsalforn. Year after year, over 65% of our clients return to dive with us again. For beginners and seasoned divers alike, diving in small groups enables our highly experienced, multilingual professional staff to provide individual guidance in a personal, friendly and helpful manner. A full range of PADI & BSAC Courses is on offer, as is guided diving from shore, from a rib (using our own fleet of trucks and our own rib) and from a hard boat.

We are a member of Quality Divers. Customer Safety is our overriding priority. We offer Nitrox for free! Gozo's dive sites are quite numerous for such a tiny island, and they vary from reefs, caverns and caves, to wrecks, drop-offs and tunnels. The underwater topography around Gozo is something spectacular and must be seen to be appreciated. Most of the dive sites are quite suitable both for the beginner and the most advanced.

The clarity of the water is rarely below 25 metres and our seas are practically free of tides and currents. Also, the water temperature is never below 14° Celsius in the winter months and reaches a maximum of 28° Celsius in the summer months. We want you to have some unforgettable diving experiences at the best dive sites in the Mediterranean! Apart from our extensive diving services, we at Calypso Dive Centre can take care of your complete holiday package including transfers, hotel accommodation, private villas with pool, self-catering apartments, guesthouses, car hire, etc. We'd love to share our passion for diving in the amazing azure waters of Gozo with you!

Extra Divers Gozo

Situated near the Grand Hotel Mgarr and established in 1999 we offer a broad range of services to our international clients.

We offer two daily dive trips, frequently additional night dives, boat trips to Comino and full day trips to Malta. Guided diving is always conducted in small groups and you will explore the most spectacular places around Gozo.

Extra Divers provides dive courses from beginner to professional level according to SSI, CMAS and PADI standards.

We offer all kinds of services - equipment rental, workshop, shop, snorkel trips, BBQs and besides that can provide you through our partners with addition services like car rental, flight booking, accommodation, transfers and organized trips around the island.

Enjoy the unique hospitality and explore the spectacular under water landscape with us.

Gaulos Dive Centre

Here at Gaulos Dive Cove, we welcome customers with a warm lovable smile; we are a small yet professional team who offer you a truly personalised diving experience. When diving with Gaulos, you'll be treated as a friend, experiencing the island on a much more intimate level. Probably why we see so many return customers!

Our instructors are patient and relaxed maintaining a fun, enjoyable atmosphere while keeping safety the top priority.

With over 15 years experience diving the islands, our crew are the ones to show you all the beauty the island hides under the water's surface. You can experience diving in the safe, clear blue waters that island offers. Our dive sites combine interesting geology, both on land and under the sea, rich diverse wildlife and habitats, dramatic seascapes dominated by a rocky shoreline along with many interesting historic backstories.

We offer diving for all levels, from beginners (without any qualification) to pros in English, Italian, Japanese and Maltese.

Included in our services is complimentary door-to-door pick-up/drop-off to our recently refurbished shop, stocked with new, top of the line equipment.

Gozo Aquasports.
PADI 5*IDC & TECREC Dive Centre & BSAC Dive Resort based in Marsalforn, Gozo. Malta.

Owned and led by Patrick Bugeja. Gozo Aqua Sports has 32 years proven experience with an unblemished safety record. By offering a personalized and friendly service we provide a tried, tested and trusted service resulting in an exceedingly high repeat customer base.

Want to find out more? Then send us an email with your requirements and let us create you a fantastic diving holiday.

Gozo Technical Divin

Located in Xewkija, the heart of Gozo and yet only 10 minutes driving from all major dive sites, Gozo Diving is a Recreational and Technical dive center (PADI IDC 5*, PADI TECREC and TDI) that offers an absolutely unique underwater exploration experience.

Our dive shop and swimming pool completes our facility which offers the latest diving equipment, any mixed gas, equipment repair and advices from professional instructors. We speak English, French, German, Spanish and Dutch. We are pioneersin developing Sidemount among other specialties such as wreck, cavern or deep diving. We train beginners and instructors up to the highest recreational and technical level. We welcome shore and boat divers as well.

Moby Dives
Moby Dives located on Malta's sister island of Gozo, is a PADI 5 STAR IDC diving school offering a whole range of PADI scuba diving courses, from Open Water all the way through to Instructor Development Courses in the most idyllic of settings. Xlendi Bay - a picturesque fishing village located on the south west coast of the island.

Combine all this with Moby Dive's excellent reputation for Scuba Training, Organisation and Professionalism whilst maintaining a friendly atmosphere with helpful Instructors and Staff. We are sure that you will have a truly memorable holiday in Gozo.

Nautic Team
Nautic Team Diving Club is situated in the beautiful island of Gozo in Marsalforn just a stone throw away from the harbor. Nautic Team Diving Club in Gozo offers diving in small groups and can take you diving in over 35 sited, just choose if you are looking for caves, grottos, tunnels, reefs, wrecks etc. To top it off, they also offer night and early morning dives as well as work-shop services, equipment rentals and sales of a variety of popular diving accessories brands.

Nautic Team Diving Club's instructors have several years of experience in diving education, individual and personal training for beginners and more advance divers and safety is the number one priority. Standards are high at this diving club and they are equipped with modern compressor facilities (BAUER and L&W) with Airlab and a KOMPTEC Membrane facility for NITROX, as well as equipment, wich meets all requirements.

Courses at Nautic Team Diving Clubcan be held according to Barakuda-CMAS, VDST, PADI and SSI standard. Junior-Courses are also available for children over 8-9 years of age.

Fortifications & Towers
Dwejra Tower
Dwejra Tower is situated just off the road leading to the small enclosed bay at Dwejra in Gozo, known as the 'inland sea'. It was completed in 1652 and periodically used by British forces up to the second World War when it was used as an observation post.

It was completed in 1652 during the time of Grand Master Jean Paul Lascaris Castellar and funded by the Universita' of Gozo. A Capo Mastro or Castellano was in charge of the Tower and raised money to cover expenses by producing salt from the salt pans in front of the Tower. In 1744 Grand Master Pinto had the sides of nearby

Fungus Rock, home of the fabled fungus that had special medicinal powers, smoothed over to make access more difficult.

The Tower was still in use during the eighteenth century when it was equipped with three 6-pounder guns. It was manned by the Royal Malta Fencible Artillery between 1839 and 1873 but then abandoned. During the summer of 1914 Maltese troops from the King's Own Malta Regiment and the Royal Malta Artillery were dispatched to the coastal watch towers and Dwejra Tower was manned by No 3 Company with two, later four, 12-pounder guns. During the Second World War the Tower was used as an Observation Post. One recorded incident was the rescue of a Royal Air Force pilot, whose Spitfire had crashed in Dwejra Bay in 1942, by Captain Frank Debono and Carmelo Zahra of Victoria.

In 1956 the Tower was leased to Gerald de Trafford for a period of fifty years. It was passed on loan to Din l-Art Helwa who commenced restoration work in 1997, which was completed two years later. A considerable amount of stonework had to be replaced on the outside and flagstones laid inside.

Tal-Ġordan Lighthouse
Għasri is home to the first lighthouse ever to be built in Gozo, known as Ta' Ġordan.

The famous lighthouse rises 180 metres above sea level and was inaugurated in 1853. Its beam can be seen up to 50 kilometres away.

Upon the hill around the lighthouse there are some marvelous 360 degree views of Gozo and this lures quite a lot of hikers, who challenge the rather steep path up to the hilltop.

The Citadel

The Citadel in Gozo owes its roots to the late medieval era, but the hill has been settled since Neolithic times.

After the Great Siege of 1565, the Knights set about re-fortifying it to provide refuge and defence against further attack.

Until 1637, the Gozitan population was required by law to spend their nights within the Citadel for their own safety.

In later, more peaceful times, this restriction was lifted and people settled below its walls, creating the prosperous town of Rabat, now known as Victoria.

Museums & Galleries

Cathedral Museum

The Gozo Cathedral Museum has more than 2000 items on display, including the Cathedral's archives, magnificent paintings, clerical vestments and a silver vault. Among the paintings are several by well-known local artists: Giuseppe Hyzler, Michele Busetti and Tommaso Medion.

Constructed between 1697 and 1711, the Cathedral is a fine Baroque structure in the form of the Latin cross and is built entirely from the local limestone. The sanctuary was built on the plans of the Maltese architect, Lorenzo Gafa. A tall belfry with five bells at the back of the Cathedral replaces the more traditional and common two belfries at the front, while a 1739 painting on the interior of the temple gives the impression of a dome, when in reality the roof of the building is flat. Another attraction of the Cathedral is the statue of Santa Marija (The Assumption of Our Lady), which was undertaken in Rome in 1897.

Folklore Museum

The exhibits displayed on the ground floor levels relate to rural trades and skills, such as agriculture and stone-masonry. Various traditional agricultural implements, including sickles, spades, winnowing forks, shovels and ploughs, together with a selection of grinding mills are on display. There are also traditional stone-dressing tools, as well as a large selection of tools used by carpenters and blacksmiths. The mezzanine floor exhibits domestic Gozitan crafts, such as lace making, weaving and bookbinding. The first floor exhibits items relating to hobbies such as hunting, as well as the modelling of miniature churches, replete with religious accessories. There is also an interesting selection of traditional costumes, a collection of elaborately worked clay statuettes, an ex-voto collection and a number of furniture items.

Gharb Folklore Museum

The Għarb Folklore Museum is a privately owned unique early 18th century historical house with 28 rooms. A tour of these rooms gives the visitor a glimpse of times gone by with exhibits such as the miller's room, an antique press room, a carpenter's workshop and a myriad of other memories from Gozo's past. The Għarb Folklore Museum (found at Pjazza Żjara tal-Madonna) is a private owned museum found in the core of the village. Its 28 rooms are full of all kind of antique tools and artifacts. It is really worth visiting.

Heart of Gozo - Il-haġar

The Basilica Museum - Il-Ħaġar | Heart of Gozo is an audio-visual, fine arts and historical museum that tells a story. It is unique in the Maltese islands in that its construction, including a medieval wing, was conceived and designed as a modern multi-mediatic museum that includes audio-visual halls and interactive points on every floor. Through the displayed objects and their ancillary information the visitors are introduced into an important aspect of Gozo: that of the island's succession of cultures, civilizations and religions, with an accent on Gozitan Christianity.

Basically this museum and cultural centre, displays a rich collection of historical and artistic artifacts previously inaccessible to the general public. There is also space for temporary exhibitions and cultural / recreational events that can be held on its panoramic roofs.

The Museum is an innovative and unique element aiding the branding of Gozo, indeed the Maltese islands, as cultural destinations of excellence.

The museum is located at St George's Square, flanking the famous and the ever popular with tourists St George's Basilica. The museum is actually conceptually and quasi-physically linked to the basilica.

Museum of Archeology
The Gozo Museum of Archaeology illustrates the cultural history of Gozo from prehistoric times to the early modern period.

The ground floor is devoted to the Neolithic Period, the Temple Period and the Bronze Age (5200-700BC), exhibiting a selection of decorated potsherds, pottery vessels, stone and bone implements and pendants from various settlements and tombs. The Bronze Age section displays a group of miniature clay containers and a decorated double-pot, as well as some fragmented clay votive anchors.

The first floor is devoted to the Phoenician, Punic, Roman, Medieval, and Knights' periods. The collections on display include jewellery, coins, marble statues, inscriptions, oil lamps and part of a limestone olive-pipper.

The collection also includes a number of inscriptions, the oldest carved in Punic characters during the second century BC to commemorate the building and restoration of sanctuaries.

Museum of Natural Science

Situated behind the law courts at the Citadel of Victoria, Gozo, the Natural Science Museum is situated in an old house, the origins of which may date back to the Aragonese period.

The geology on exhibits includes marine organisms deposited on the sea floor between 35 and 5 million years ago, as well as fragments of fossil bones from Ice Age elephants and hippopotami. The centrepiece is a selection of stalactites and stalagmites from Gozitan caves.

Two other sections on this floor are dedicated to human and animal evolution as well as marine life.

The second floor exhibits an ornithology display; a small collection of stuffed and mounted birds, the majority of which are migratory and most of which are now legally protected species.

The entomology room holds a small but impressive collection of exotic insects, butterflies and moths.

The last display is dedicated to the flora and ecosystems of the Maltese Islands, particularly of Gozo.

Museum of Toys
This small privately owned museum in Xaghra was originally set up by Susan Lowe in Devon, England in the 1970's. It started with one doll and today it boasts toys from all around the world. The name Pomzkizillious comes from Edward Lear who made up this word to describe the coastal scenery of Gozo while visiting the Island in 1866. (Edward Lear is a world famous illustrator of natural history

books, writer & illustrator of children's verse and a landscape painter who visited Malta on many occasions)

The earliest objects on display are a late 18th century Maltese Doll with carved wooden head and some Italian Presepio and figurines dating from 1790's. Among other attractions there is a 1930's Noah's Ark, a "Hornby" Train Set and Edwin's "Dinky" vehicles, a pressed paper "Hunting Scene" & "Zoo" which have survived over 100 years and a set of soldiers made in the 1970's but dressed in the uniform of the Swedish Army in 1700's. A scarce set of unmarked Lead Cricketers and other lead toys including Zoo & Farm Animals, Cowboys & Indians, Aeroplanes, Ships & Soldiers and an Ambulance Set about 1890's are also on display.

One can also see some optical toys, 1790's dolls, soft toys made by Steiff, Lenci and Kathe Kruse, and a few clockwork tin toys from the 1920/30's (Schuco & Lehmann).

Old Prison
Situated in the Citadel in Victoria, Gozo the Old Prison lies adjacent to the Courts of Justice to which it was originally connected. In its present form, the prison complex is divided into two sections: the entrance hall which served as a common cell in the 19th century and now hosts a permanent exhibition on fortifications and a free-

standing block with six individual cells. Having undergone a number of structural modifications, this prison was in use from the mid-16th century until the beginning of the 20th century.

Soon after their arrival in Malta, the Knights of St John used this prison to intern their rowdy and disruptive members. The list of notorious inmates included Fra Jean Parisot de La Valette (later, Grand Master of Malta) who, in 1538, spent four months in the Gozo prison after having attacked a man.

After the expulsion of the Knights of St John from Malta, the prison remained in use. From the mid-19th century, another building on the other side of the Citadel started functioning as a prison and continued to serve this purpose until it closed down in 1962. Initially, the new prison was in use simultaneously with the old one which, for some decades, continued to house those individuals awaiting trial.

The walls of the cells and corridors in the Old Prison are covered with graffiti. This is the largest known collection of historical graffiti in one single place on the Maltese Islands. They include mainly sea vessels and date from different periods. But there are also palm-prints, crosses, names, dates, games, and anthropomorphic figures. Some inmates also appear to have scratched a tally of their length of stay behind bars. These graffiti provide a fascinating insight into the lives of those incarcerated here.

Ta` Kola Windmill

The Ta' Kola windmill is a step back in time to the trade of the miller and a fine example of the rural economy and domestic life of Gozo in centuries past.

Built in 1725 and named after the miller who lived and worked here (in Maltese 'mithna' means windmill and ta' Kola means 'of Nicholas' - Nicholas' Windmill). The mill consists of a rectangular building that incorporates a circular tower some 15 metres high. Of the twelve windmills built by the Knights, only the Ta' Kola windmill in Gozo still remains in good working condition. The windmill is now available to show visitors how these mills worked.

The Museum also houses a wide range of tools, some of which were originally manufactured by the owners of the mill.

On the first floor, the living quarters of the miller have been recreated using traditional furniture and items related to Gozitan crafts, such as weaving and lace making.

Natural Attractions

Calypso's Cave

This cave is situated in a cliff face, a short distance from Xaghra and overlooks the red sands of Ramla Bay.

This cave is assumed to be the cave referred to by Homer in `The Odyssey' where Calypso, the beautiful nymph kept Odysseus as a `prisoner of love' for seven years.

The cave's interior and exterior are not too impressive but the magnificent views are worth it.

Fungus Rock

Fungus Rock and the Inland Sea are two spectacular natural landmarks in Dwejra.

Fungus Rock - known in Maltese as Il-Gebla Tal-General (or General's Rock) is a small islet in the form of a 60 metres high massive lump of limestone situated right at the entrance to an almost circular lagoon.

During the times of the Knights, it was thought that a particular tuber which grows on this little island had medicinal properties and could cure various ailments. So much so that the Grandmaster declared it illegal for anyone other than authorised knights to climb onto the rock and pick the plant, Today, tests are being conducted to verify whether these medical claims have any foundation

Inland Sea

The Inland Sea is an inland lagoon in Dwejra, and is perhaps the archipelago's most spectacular natural landmark.

The Inland Sea, and Dwejra Bay itself, were created millions of years ago when two limestone caves collapsed. The shallow inland lagoon is linked to the sea via a 100 metre cave in the cliff. On calm days, small fishing boats carry visitors out to sea through this tunnel, in order to see Fungus Rock and the spectacular cliffs in the area. The sea is used by fishermen and bathers, and is also a very popular diving spot.

Overlooking the lagoon is the Chapel of St. Anne, built in 1963 on the site of a much older church.

Saltpans

Saltpans are one of the most interesting features of the Maltese coastline.

Found practically all around the islands' shoreline, these shallow repositories dug out of the rock were common even in Roman times, and the technology has not changed much since then. The pans are used to collect sea water which is gradually dried up by the sun, to leave a white residue. This is then collected, cleaned and refined to produce sea salt.

Some of the best saltpans (and certainly the most photographed) are the ones located at Qbajjar, near Marsalforn in Gozo

Ta' Mena Agritourism

At Ta' Mena Estate, you will find yourself immersed in the typical Gozitan country-side, surrounded by a natural and calm environment, and breathtaking views.

The estate is situated in the picturesque Marsalforn Valley between Victoria and Marsalforn Bay. It includes a fruit garden, an olive grove with about 1500 olive trees, an orange grove, and over ten hectares of vineyards. It enjoys the panoramic views of the Gozo Citadel and the surrounding hills and villages.

At Ta' Mena Estate we cultivate vines, olives, lemons, oranges, various fruit trees, strawberries, tomatoes, melons, water melons and other vegetables. We produce our own wine in a state of the art winery, press our olives to produce a unique cold pressed extra virgin olive oil in our modern olive press and produce various typical liqueurs and foods from our different fruit, vegetables and herbs. Our sundried tomato paste is a must to try!

We also organise wedding and anniversary receptions, guided tours around the estate followed by wine and food tasting, cooking sessions complete with lunch or dinner, barbeques, picnics and hands-on agricultural experiences including strawberry and fruit picking, grape and olive harvesting and on site experiences of wine-making and olive-oil pressing.

We are setting up an agricultural heritage museum covering Gozitan rural life throughout the ages. Our farm with indigenous domestic animals is taking shape and will be used as a patting farm especially for children. We offer ample areas for children to play around, organise pony rides, horse-riding tours, hikes, jeep safaris and private boat rides around Gozo and Comino.

The estate offers a holiday with a difference with its particular spots, self catering apartments and typical rustic farmhouses completed with all amenities and private swimming pools. We guarantee that your holiday will be unique, far away from the complicated and stressful daily life of the modern era. You will relax and revitalize yourself while savoring some of the Mediterranean history and nature at its best.

Xerri's Grotto

Discovered in 1923, this cave is known for its strange and colourful alabaster stalactites and stalagmites.

The Grotto is to be found at a depth of 9 meters and the entrance is via a spiral stone staircase. The owners normally give a quick tour pointing out the unusual geological forms created over the millennia. Part of the excavations was carried out during the Second World War when the owning family used the cave as an air raid shelter

Shopping

Arkadia Commercial Centre

Arkadia Commercial Centre is Gozo's leading shopping destination situated on your entry into Victoria. From fashion to home to food, you will find all you need from Arkadia. Within the commercial centre visitors can find a fully serviced foodstore with a butcher, delicatessen, fishmonger, as a well as a dedicated fresh fruit and vegetable section. Arkadia is also home to McDonalds and McCafe in Gozo. Visitors can also find several reknown fashion brands such as Tommy Hilfigger, Miss Selfridge, Suiteblanco, Pimkie, Orsay, Peacocks, Parfois, Piazza Italia, Next, amongst others.

Savina Creations

Make your trip to Gozo truly memorable. Visit Savina Creations Limited and get all the tips you need before setting off to explore the Island of Gozo.

At Savina you will witness food in-the-making of a vast range of products produced here, from home-made chutneys, honey and jams to olives, antipasti, pickles, pâtés, tea and coffee. The recipes are typically Mediterranean and a feast for your senses. Savina's products make excellent gifts to take back home - either for friends and dear ones, or simply to enjoy yourself! A selection of Christmas hampers is already available, however, there's nothing quite like a bespoke, fine food hamper with over 150 exclusive items to choose from!

We promise to excel in the creation of innovative and customised gifts that offer pleasure to our worldwide customers, drawing on Magro Brothers' belief and expertise for providing quality, premium Maltese and Mediterranean specialties and make this for the benefit of the community at large.

At the Savina Centre you will able to sample food and dairy products which are well-liked by both locals and visitors. If you have any questions, you can ask the staff as they are very knowledgeable in their work, and obviously you may also opt to take a product home with you to remind you of Gozo's tastes and traditions.

Ta' Dbieġi Crafts Village
The crafts village in Gozo is located in the oldest village of the island, also known as Gharb on the west close to the famous Ta' Pinu Shrine. This craft village is very well laid out with individual shops scattered around the site. When visiting the Ta' Dbiegi Craft Village in Gozo, you can see hand-made pottery, Gozo lace, glass blowing and leather items. In Maria's lace shop you can see a fascinating demonstration on how lace is done, something that should not to be missed.

Visiting the Ta' Dbiegi Craft Village in Gozo gives you the unique opportunity to buy handmade lace and other items which are perfect souvenirs and gifts to take back home to family and friends. If you visit this craft village, ensure that you also visit the Gharb Folklore Museum and the Ta' Pinu Shrine.

The Duke Shopping Centre
The Duke Shopping Mall offers all the requisites to make it stand out from other shopping centres in Gozo, being the only mall that boasts state-of-the-art resi¬dential, office and shopping outlets. Located within easy reach from the bus terminal and the

surrounding four parking areas, the building also boasts its customer car park.

Open since November 2008, The Duke has continuously undergone growth, with the first expansion occurring in October 2009, when Benetton, Playlife and Sisley opened shop in a 400-square-metre area.

By the end of 2010 and throughout 2011, a perfumery, a toyshop and a household outlet by TKS Home opened on Level -1. Promod, Kappa, Mamas & Papas, Eurosport and Reebok Fitness were added in level 0. In November 2012, Bortex joined the group.

Today, the mall is home to over 24 retail outlets, including Monsoon Kids, Accessorize, Adidas, Artigli, Bortex, E-Jewels, Piccinino, TipTop Electronics, Reebok, Reebok Fitness, Kappa, Eurosport, Mamas & Papas, Fergi, Pumpkin Patch, Bata, Skechers, Promod, Benetton, Playlife, Sisley, Chemimart, TKS Home and Toyworld.

To complement these renowned brands, Salus offers a beauty and hair care salon, while a fully-fledged food store is set on an area of 1,150 square metres, offering advantageous prices and special offers to its customers. Finally, there's also Connection Cafe, which is considered as the place to be in Gozo.

Tiġrija Palazz Shopping Centre

Tigrija Palazz is situated at the cross roads of Gozo, precisely at the corner where the roads lead you to the picturesque bays of Xlendi, Marsalforn and Dwejra. Tigrija Palazz is only 10 minutes walk away from Victoria's main parking lot and the bus terminus. This position makes Tigrija Palazz the ideal on stop complex for all your shopping needs.

There are 33 shopping outlets and one bistro. In fact the complex holds a variety mix of shopping and service outlets providing the customers with;

Food
- ✓ Various fashion brands and accessories
- ✓ Beauty products
- ✓ Opticians
- ✓ Gifts & jewelry
- ✓ Café
- ✓ Books and stationery
- ✓ Mobile phones and DVD rentals

- ✓ A fitness centre service
- ✓ Bank and business services as well as;
- ✓ Tourist information services.

Facilitie

Gozo Sports Complex

At the Gozo Sports Complex they aim to achieve the highest standards where sports activities in Gozo are concerned.

Their commitment to their clients is to serve all members of the community by providing sports facilities for up to 23 different kinds of sports.

Gozo Stadium

The Gozo Stadium, formerly known as the Silver Jubilee Ground, is the national stadium of the island of Gozo, Malta. The Gozo Stadium stages matches of the highest division in Gozo, part of the Second Division League and the matches of the Gozo F.C. It approximately holds 4,000 people. It is divided into two sides: the Xewkija side and the Xagħra side. The Xewkija Side is the enclosure area and in the middle, where one can find the VIP area. The Gozo Stadium, to date is the only stadium with natural grass pitch found on the Maltese island of Gozo.

Despite its limited budget, recently a lot of work is being done in order to improve the facilities at the stadium. The main mission of the new board of the GFA is to improve the facilities of the Gozo Stadium in order to reach UEFA and FIFA standards so in the future the stadium could host international matches of the Maltese National Team.

Gun Blast Shooting Range

The Gun Blast Shooting Range is a newly born shooting organisation, which is the first legal shooting range in Gozo. Target shooting is a unique and exciting sport which is enjoyed by the young and old alike in the Maltese Islands.

Major goals of the organisation are to promote and mange the development of amateur sport shooters in the country. The organisation is authorised for training and to organize and supervise shooting competitions on a local and national level.

Service Providers

Gozo Adventure

Gozo Adventures is a company specialised in organising Kayaking, Biking, Climbing, Hiking and Adventure Tours in Gozo.

Kayaking:

Explore Gozo and Comino's varied coastline by kayak and enjoy the islands stunning scenery from a different and peaceful perspective.

Our kayak tours allow visitors to explore Gozo and Comino's caves and bays using muscle power rather than polluting petrol, and also to get up close to dramatic limestone cliffs and marine life.

At Gozo Adventures all of our kayak tours are led by fully trained sea kayak instructors and we use high quality equipment to offer enjoyable and safe experiences for our guests.

We work with the weather - starting trips from the most suitable side of the island each day, and adapt the tours to suit experience levels. We paddle to the famous Blue Lagoon out of season when tourist boats are scarce, and avoid the same site when it is overcrowded in summer seeking out more private spots to stop. Our guides are knowledgeable about the local geography and sea life and point out things of interest en route.

We offer 1/2 day tours for €45pp and full days at €65pp. Our full day is usually from 9.30 till 16.00 and our half-day is offered at the end of our full day from 16.30 till 19.30. Our price includes an experienced guide, kayaks and safety equipment and for the full day, also a picnic lunch. To run this tour a minimum of 2 guests is required (3 guests for the ½ day). Contact us for family and group discounts.

Climbing:
If you are looking to go climbing on Gozo, then look no further! Whether you are a beginner, looking to move from indoor to outdoor climbing, or already an experience climber, Gozo has a number of inland crags and sea cliff routes to suit your needs and desires.

Gozo Adventures climbing and abseiling tours make the most of Gozo's natural dry and rocky landscape without the need to alter it in any way. The limestone rock formations and the mild climate between October to May provides Gozo with a natural adventure playground well suited for climbing and abseiling! There is also an indoor bouldering facility in the Gozo Sports Complex in Victoria that is available for public use all year round.

At Gozo Adventures our guides will take you to the best locations on the island to suit your experience and needs. They are also happy to extend your skills by combing your climbing day with abseiling and with technique and skills development. Experience the fun and thrill of descending and climbing cliffs and tackle progressively larger climbs as your ability and confidence grows.

A full day climbing is € 65 per person and a half day is € 45. It includes an experienced guide, all the equipment and safety equipment and a picnic lunch (on full day tour). To run this tour a minimum of 2 guests is required (3 guests for the ½ day).Contact us for family and groups discounts

Biking:
Biking in Gozo is becoming a popular activity with locals and visitors alike. The islands have a great deal to offer a cyclist, with long country roads, narrow walled streets with rough surfaces and smooth long stretches that allow you to get into a good rhythm. Gozo's national symbol is the three hills, and even though the highest point of the island is no greater than 450 meters above sea level there are a great number of cycling routes that offering physical and technical challenges.

The best months for mountain biking in Gozo are the mild winter months from October to May. when the island is a lush green carpet of wild flowers and herbs and temperatures are lower - however biking is possible all year round.

At Gozo Adventures our guides do their best to choose routes that take in your interests and cater for your ability level. Rather than whizzing along the main roads in a car, our bike routes take you through the countryside, along picturesque roads and valleys with stunning views and past historical temple sites and other places of interest

We also have downhill routes which take in a variety of landscapes at a more relaxed pace!

A full day Biking is € 65 per person and a half day is € 45. This includes a guide, all the equipment and safety equipment and a picnic lunch (on full day tour). To run this tour a minimum of 2 guests is required (3 guests for the ½ day). Contact us for family and group discounts.

Gozo Adventures - Adventure Day Tour
This tour allows you to pick different activities to suit your interests and the time of year.
Choose two from the four activities listed below to experience in one day.
Climbing and abseiling
Adventure hiking
Mountain biking
Swimming and snorkelling
During the summer months, it is a good idea to try climbing and abseiling in the morning shade and spend the afternoon swimming and snorkeling.

From October to May it becomes a little cold for swimming, but we can offer any combination of the other three activities.

An Adventure Day is € 65 per person. It includes transport, an experienced guide, all the equipment and safety equipment and a picnic lunch. To run this tour a minimum of 2 guests is required. Half day with one activity can be offered with a minimum of 3 guests. Contact us for family and group discounts.

Eco Tour

The Gozo Adventures Eco tour will take you away from the usual tourist sites to show you the places and people we know and love. This tour is entirely reliant on the skills and friendliness of the people of Gozo! Rather than the usual tour guide format where guests are "told" information - this tour introduces you to a variety of local people in their everyday work and play settings. You have the opportunity to ask questions directly to these local experts - and we're never quite sure how they will react!

We don't like to give away too many details of this day to keep the element of surprise.

We will however tell you that the day includes a large focus on traditional foods with opportunities to do more that just eat it for lunch (although that bit alone is worth coming for!). The day also gives you opportunities to interact with local people other than hotel or restaurant staff, learn a little about every day life and traditions and learn a new game.

Interaction between tourists and locals helps visitors to understand more about Gozo. However, at a time of globalisation when many traditional skills are being lost, the interest and admiration of visitors for these traditional ways of life helps to foster a sense of pride amongst the Gozitan people which we hope will help to keep these skills alive.

The Gozo Adventures Eco tour costs € 75 per person and includes a guide, all transport, meetings and experiences with a range of local people, and a restaurant meal (traditional Gozitan lunch) with wine. To run the tour a minimum of 6 people is required.

Theatre & Opera
Astra Theatre
Local talent is extensively featured and encouraged with special prominence to operas. Visiting companies are also notably presented on the Astra stage and most of the major theatrical companies in Malta have performed at the theatre at one time or another.

Oratorju Don Bosco

Don Bosco Oratory in Saint Augustine Square was officially opened on the 8th October 1949. The cinema was inaugurated in May 1951 and showed movies uninterruptedly until 1986 when dwindling audiences meant that it was no longer feasible to run the cinema. In early nineties, Malta saw the opening of new cinemas equipped with the latest technology and comfort. These were instrumental in encouraging people back to the cinemas. The Don Bosco Oratory followed suit and on Sunday the 6th of February 1994 opened the cinema doors again with the movie 'Home Alone 2 - Lost In New York'. Today, movies at Oratory Don Bosco are shown every Sunday between October and May at 17.30. From time to time, movies are shown on different occasions, including special screenings for school children and other groups.

The Oratorju Don Bosco is also well known for its theatrical productions and family shows

Towns & Villages
Fontana

Fontana, locally known simply as 'Triq tal-Għajn', (the way to the spring), took its name from a bountiful spring at the bottom of the road leading to Xlendi, locally referred to as 'il-Għajn il-Kbira', (the big spring).

Fontana, a suburb of Victoria, lies downhill on the Rabat-Xlendi road. People began to inhabit the area because of this useful fresh water springs. The arched shelters were built in the sixteenth century over each spring for the convenience of the people. Inside one can still find traditional stone water tubs in which local folk could do their daily washing.

On the lower part of Fontana, on the right-hand side of the road to Xlendi, one could not help but notice the evergreen Lunzjata Valley going up to the village of Ta' Kerċem. Local farmers busy around all year long in this fertile part of Gozo.

Ghajnsielem

Għajnsielem is a village situated in the South East of Gozo.

As soon as you enter Mġarr Harbour, while still aboard the ferry, you could not help but notice the welcoming landmarks of this harbour village. Its name originated from the water spring, around which in 1700, Grandmaster Perellos built an arcade containing public washbasins and fresh water spouts. So without any stretch of imagination, the name Għajnsielem means "a peaceful spring".

According to a well known legend, the village's "founding father" Anġlu Grech had a 'vision' of Our Lady near the spring and was directed to erect a statue of Our Lady of Loreto at a specified place near the spring. The statue was erected, and later, the church followed suit.

In Għajnsielem there is Fort Chambray, built after 1749, which offered security to the inhabitants of the area. The village has a number of other historical and archaeological attractions. These include the Mġarr ix-Xini Tower and the larger Saint Cecilia Tower which is located near the main road leading to Xewkija. Near St. Cecilia Tower (built in 1618) one can still get a glimpse of the ancient chapel dedicated to the same saint and which is, reputedly, the oldest chapel on the island.

A unique Neolithic settlement, also in this outlying part of Għajnsielem, was excavated by a team of archaeologists from Cambridge University in 1987.

Gharb

Għarb means West and this typical old Gozitan village unsurprisingly lies in the West of the Island.

It started life as a small hamlet centuries ago. You can see its ancient roots in the centre of the village where some houses have fine example of decorated stone balconies. Għarb was created a parish in 1679, a move which gave impetus for the building of a new, baroque parish church. Built between 1699 and 1729, it has an elegant facade which has been compared with Borromini's S. Agnese in Piazza Navona, Rome. This version is naturally a simpler interpretation of the style. The village square, so quintessentially Gozitan, has become the view on many a postcard. On the square is a fascinating folklore museum housing all sorts of memorabilia retelling the Islands' rural history. Għarb lies in some of Gozo's most delightful countryside, particularly at Dbiegi, the highest hill on the Island. Also at Dbiegi is a crafts village.

Within the limits of Għarb is the quaint Chapel of San Dimitri. According to legend, the first chapel was built on the cliff side by a woman whose son was freed from captivity by St. Demetrius. Also nearby is the Basilica ta' Pinu, Malta's pre-eminent shrine to the Virgin Mary. It was on this spot in 1883 that a local woman is believed to have heard the voice of the Virgin.

Discovering Malta & Gozo Through its People & Culture

A project initiated by the Ministry for Tourism, the Environment and Culture in 2011 has led to the development of a number of itineraries for villages and towns which are considered to be on the periphery with regard to mainstream tourism, but which nonetheless showcase the real and authentic experience of the Maltese Islands.

Għasri

Għasri is Gozo's smallest parish and village, and one of the most traditional.

Like neighbouring Żebbuġ, with which it formed part till 1921, Għasri probably owes its name to the olive industry. The village of Għasri leads to Għasri Vslley, which ends in a beautiful tight gorge, dropping into the sea.

Għasri is home to the first lighthouse ever to be built in Gozo, known as Ta' Ġordan. The famous lighthouse rises 180 metres above sea level and was inaugurated in 1853. Its beam can be seen up to 50 kilometres away. Upon the hill around the lighthouse there are some marvelous 360 degree views of Gozo and this lures quite a lot of hikers, who challenge the rather steep path up to the hilltop.

From the Village Square, a road leads to the fabulous valley of Wied il-Għasri. On the way, there are a number of typical farmhouses, most of them available for short or long lets, as well as an old charming chapel dedicated to the Patronage of the Blessed Virgin Mary.

The Wied il-Għasri area is a marvelous country walk or cycling site especially in Winter and Spring.

Marsalforn

Marsalforn, meaning 'bakery harbour', is Gozo's main seaside town. During the summer, it becomes a bustling, lively resort. There is a small but pleasant sandy bank on the harbour with safe bathing and good rocky coastline towards Qbajjar which is excellent for snorkelling.

The resort has a good range of accommodation from seafront self-catering apartments to hotels. Marsalforn is characterised by its harbour-side cafes and restaurants, many serving fresh fish. The small harbour is the main port for a fleet of traditional 'luzzijiet' trawlers and smaller fishing boats. The beauty of Marsalforn is its relaxed atmosphere, even in the height of summer.

Mġarr Harbour

Besides being Gozo's main harbour, Mġarr is one of the most important fishing villages of the Island, providing the best shelter for the local fishing boats during the winter months.

Mġarr also boasts a modern yacht marina which hosts a large number of yachts and pleasure boats throughout the year.

The fishing port is a hive of activity throughout the year with fishermen either preparing their equipment for the fishing season or returning to harbour to sell their catch.

Overlooking Mġarr Harbour is Fort Chambrai, which was built by the Knights of St. John in 1749 and later used by the British forces. A church dedicated to Our Lady of Lourdes also overlooks Mġarr.

Typical of Mediterranean fishing ports, the harbour is very well served with restaurants and bars.

Munxar

The village of Munxar lies to the South of the island of Gozo, between Xlendi Valley and the village of Sannat.

Wedged between the sloping sides of two parallel valleys Munxar offers some of the most beautiful landscapes in Gozo. Munxar derives from Arabic meaning bucksaw, a description perhaps of the sheer rock faces of the scenic gorge nearby which seem deliberately cut out of the countryside. The ravine was in fact a river bed in the ice age. The village itself has numerous links with the sea, although it lies safely inland. The parish church is dedicated to the Islands' most famous shipwreck, that of St. Paul in A.D. 60. Munxar only became a parish in 1957 and remains a quiet village tucked away inland from its livelier sister village, the resort of Xlendi Bay.

Also worth mentioning are the remnants of a prehistoric temple at Ta' Marziena in Munxar. However, although these temples date approximately to the Ġgantija period, they were not as appropriately excavated and could not be appreciated by anyone less than an archaeological expert.

Nadur

Nadur lies on the hills above a fertile valley, once the hunting grounds of Grand Master Wignacourt but now the fruit growing district of the Island.

Nadur has grown so fast in recent times that it is considered Gozo's second town. The baroque Parish Church dominates Nadur's skyline and is believed to be one of Gozo's best baroque architectural masterpieces. This church dedicated to St. Peter and St. Paul was designed in 1766 . The facade and dome make it one the most grand and monumental of Gozo's churches. The village is renowned for its Carnival, which unlike the more festive occasions in other locations takes on a sombre and dark mood because of the macabre costumes. Nadur Carnival is a unique experience. It is so unique for the spontaneity and creativity of all those taking part.

Nadur also includes the coastal area of San Blas, and Daħlet Qorrot - both are small coves perfect for snorkelling. Some of the ledges and small caves at Daħlet Qorrot have been converted into boat houses and summer retreats for local people. From Nadur you can also reach Gozo's largest and prettiest sandy bay, Ir-Ramla. The craggy heights of Nadur were an excellent viewpoint to spot any marauding armies or pirate raiders. The name Nadur means 'look out' in Maltese, but the landmark Kenuna Tower was not built for defensive reasons - it was a telegraph link between Gozo and Malta.

The village has a maritime museum which houses an interesting collection of naval artifacts from the old Nadur trade of seafaring. Visiting the Kelinu Grima Maritime Museum is really worthwhile.

Qala
Qala is the eastern-most point of Gozo and the village the furthest from the capital Victoria.

It lies near some spectacular coastline and offers clear views of Comino and Malta. Except for a few sheltered inlets such as Hondoq ir-Rummien, a secluded bathing spot, the coastline is rocky but it offers excellent walking country. Breathtaking scenes can be enjoyed from the Qala belvedere and from the small courtyard in front of a church dedicated to the immaculate conception. This Sanctuary has been a place of pilgrimage for centuries, certainly since Norman times. The area has many sites of historical and rural interest. The coastline here has several examples of one of the Knights most bizarre weapons, the `fougasse' - a primitive mortar fired from a rock-cut shaft.

Other sites include the salt pans, the Islands' best preserved windmill, and prehistoric remains. The archaeological sites dates back to the temple period and Punic-Romano pottery sherds have been found here. A large slab, roughly the shape of a pyramid, may have been the cornerstone of a temple. It is known in Gozitan mythology as the seat of a giantess.

San Lawrenz
San Lawrenz is a small hilltop village near some of the Gozo's most spectacular coastline at Dwejra.

The village is characterised by 17th century houses, many with elaborately carved stone balconies. Its parish church was built around 120 years ago in baroque style. It contains many beautiful works of art by well-known local artists such as Guiseppe Cali'. The area around San Lawrenz records almost all periods in the Islands' history. Archaeological remains include another set of the Islands' enigmatic, prehistoric 'cart ruts'; evidence of a Carthaginian temple; and a Roman tomb.

From the time of the Knights comes the legendary Fungus Rock at Dwejra. Few rocks can claim such historical importance as this giant. It is home to a plant, mistakenly called a fungus, which was reputed to have exceptional healing powers. It was so prized by the Knights used Dwejra Tower, built in 1651 as part of the line of coastal watch towers, to protect the rock and guard the plant for their use only.

At Dwejra too is the Inland Sea, a shallow inlet with a small tunnel through the rock face as access to the sea.

The Dwejra coastline is embedded with fossils, which include the teeth of enormous shark from the Miocene period.

Santa Luċija

The village of Santa Luċija lies to the west of Victoria, the capital city of Gozo and right next door to Ta' Kerċem.

It is one of the greenest areas on Gozo and was once known for its fresh water springs. The church dedicated to St. Lucy, was first recorded in 1575, and rebuilt from its foundations in the 1790's. The latest development took place in 1950. The village square is marked by a traditional stone cross. Santa Luċija (St. Lucy) is invoked by those who have problems with their eyesight. The feast day is on December 13th.

In 2008, the locality of Santa Luċija was awarded the title of European Destination of Excellence.

Ta' Kerċem
Although only a short distance from the Island's capital, Victoria, Ta' Kerċem is a secluded village.

Ta' Kerċem's origins are ancient: in fact, the village and the outlying countryside are home to several antiquities, and the source of much Gozitan folklore. Il-Mixta hill nearby is thought to be the site of the first human habitation of the Maltese Islands. In the village, you can see the remnants of its ancient past - an old windmill cum defensive tower; and some stone balconies depicting the oriental crescent or half-moon. The parish church is a relatively recent replacement (1851) of an older chapel.

The sister village of Santa Luċija though has a quaint chapel built in 1657. The square here is marked by a traditional stone cross. The countryside beyond both villages is breathtaking. The cliffs nearby are as spectacular as those at Dingli in Malta. The area was once known for its fresh water springs and is still the most lush area of Gozo. You can still see parts of an acquaduct built by the British in 1839 which carried water to Victoria.

The nearby Lunzjata Valley was once a hunting ground for the Knights. In the valley is the Chapel of the Annuniciation, tucked under a cliff. It is one of the most ancient in Gozo and dates back to 1347.

Ta' Sannat

Even today, you may still chance across women sitting at their door steps working the bobbins, though this outdoor socialising and working has all but died out. The village leads to Gozo's highest cliffs, Ta' Ċenċ, some 130 metres high. The cliffs were important in the times of the Knights as they provided an excellent breeding ground for their Peregrine hunting falcons. The cliffs today are home to a large colony of Corry Sheerwaters; the last falcons died out in the 1980s. The cliff top is home to some enigmatic archaeological sites. The prehistoric `cart ruts', parallel tracks hewn in the rock, are so close to the edge as to defy logic. On the plateau overlooking the village lie the remains of a temple and further along are several menhirs, or standing stones, thought to be a kind of megalithic `painting gallery', the only one of its kind on the Islands. In the village itself you can see traces of its ancient origins. Several stone balconies are in Moorish style. One of the few archaeological remains from Arabic times, a grave stone, was found in the Sannat area, close to Xewkija. The village also has a remarkable number of religious niches.

Victoria

All roads in Gozo lead to Rabat, also known as Victoria. The village's Citadel is visible from almost all the Island, rising steeply above the surrounding countryside.

The Citadel in Gozo owes its roots to the late medieval era, but the hill has been settled since Neolithic times. For centuries, the Citadel served as a sanctuary from attack by Barbary corsairs and Saracens. At several times during Gozo's history, these raiders took its population into slavery.

After the Great Siege of 1565, the Knights set about re-fortifying the Citadel to provide refuge and defence against further attack. Until 1637, the Gozitan population was required by law to spend their nights within the Citadel for their own safety. In later, more peaceful times, this restriction was lifted and people settled below its walls, creating the prosperous town of Rabat, now known as Victoria.

Victoria is not just the geographic heart of Gozo, it is also the centre of everyday activity. It manages to combine the bustle of its market and shops with a relaxed and sociable atmosphere. It is a great place to watch the Islanders go about their day, especially when the main market square, It-Tokk, comes to life.

Browse around Victoria's market and narrow winding streets and you'll find everything from delicious fresh produce, cheeses and wines, to antiques, craft goods, fishing nets and knitwear. The town also has a thriving cultural life all its own, with some surprising attractions ranging from opera to horse races in the main street on festa day.

Xaghra

Apart from being in itself a picturesque village, the village of Xagħra is rich in historical heritage and therefore has plenty to offer to its visitors.

Situated on the north east of the capital town of Victoria, on a lengthy stretch of high ground, Xagħra is encircled by the beautiful bays. Xagħra is famous for the prehistoric sites, the temples of Ġgantija. Calypso's cave, of mythical fame, also lies within Xagħra. The present village has a more recent history. It became a parish in 1688, but the main church was only built during the mid 19th century. It is one of the most beautiful of Gozo's churches, with its richly-decorated interior, gilt sculptures, Italian marbles and paintings.

The village also has two curious grottos, Ta' Xerri and Ta' Ninu, both of them beneath private houses but open to the public. The grottos have remarkable stalactites and stalagmites. The village also has two unusual museums: a Toy Museum; and an old wheat-grinding windmill. The mill, still in working order, has been fully restored and houses a collection of agricultural and domestic artefacts from centuries past.

Xewkija
Xewkija lies in the middle between Mġarr Harbour and Victoria.

Xewkija is dominated by a huge rotunda church completed in 1971 after some 20 years building. It is Gozo's answer to the Mosta Rotunda in Malta, and it was built in similar fashion, over an earlier, 17th century church which was only demolished at the last. The dome is larger than St. Paul's Cathedral in London. The church has capacity for a congregation of 3000, the entire population of Xewkija. It was funded entirely by local donation and built mainly with labour from the village. The interior is stark and plain in comparison to the Islands' usual baroque decoration, but is spectacular for its cavernous size. A small museum houses relics and paintings from the earlier church.

The village has ancient roots despite its modern image. It was the first parish outside the capital and according to legend the first place on Gozo to convert to Christianity. The area was settled by the Arabs. A remnant of Arab culture in the whereabouts of Xewkija is the renowned marble slab of Majmuna (pron. Maimoona) with an inscription in Arabic dating back to 1173. The slab is the tombstone of an Arab girl named Majmuna, who died and was buried in the area between Xewkija and Sannat. Today the Majmuna Stone is one of the most highly cherished historical treasures in our islands and could be found in the Museum of Archaeology in Victoria. The Arab influence lasted well into the time of the Knights - several balconies on 17th century houses are in the richly-carved Moorish style.

The landscape around Xewkija has evidence of earlier times. The deep, scenic gorge, known as Mġarr ix-Xini, was cut by a prehistoric river. This natural landmark leads to a small inlet which was used by the Knights as a galley harbour. They built a tower on the headland to defend their base. Today, Mġarr ix-Xini is relatively quiet bathing spot with a small, shingle beach.

Xlendi

The idyllic landlocked bay of Xlendi and the glorious blue green waters were for many years a haunt of artists and photographers.

The delightful sea inlet, known as Xlendi Bay, lies at the end of a deep, lush ravine which was a river bed. Until the mid 20th century, Xlendi was a small fishing port and a restful summer resort for a few locals and Maltese. The bay is now on the must-visit list of most day-trippers to the Island, but if staying on Gozo, it is a worthwhile visit. Gozo has its passionate admirers and Xlendi is , and has always been a must visit when on Gozo. Unlike Marsalforn with its resorty air, Xlendi is popular in the old sense of the word. With its precipitous sides, Xlendi is an overall beautiful place . Its watchtower commands the bays entrance, yet everybody is invited! The bathing all around the bay is possible and good fun.

The Bay of Xlendi still retains a peaceful atmosphere and is surprisingly undeveloped though there is a good choice of accommodation from apartments to hotels; most options have sea views. Xlendi is flanked by steep cliff. For some of the best views, climb the stairs up the cliffs to the right. Bathing in Xlendi is usually off the rocks along the bay with access down ladder into the deep crystal clear water. On the left side of the bay, two tiers of pathways provide ample space for both a walkway and a flat space to spread out a towel and sunbathe.

On the promontory is Xlendi Tower, built in 1650. It commands superb sea views and stands on a scenic coastline pitted with hand-dug salt pans.More recently it has very much become a tourist resort. The single beach , rocky shore and clear waters are good for swimming and the caves and rugged reefs provide ideal conditions for snorkeling and scuba diving. Some of the restaurants on the seafront specialize in local fish and succulent giant prawns.

Żebbuġ

This picturesque village, perched on one of Gozo's highest hills, offers spectacular sea views and panoramas over the Island with some of the best views of Ċittadella.

In centuries past, olive trees were cultivated on the hills where the village stands. Its name, meaning olives, recalls the fact. Żebbuġ is an ancient village. It became a parish in 1688 and its baroque church dates from 1736. As is typical of many Gozitan villages, the streets in the centre are narrow and winding. Żebbuġ is noted for a special marble quarried nearby: the material is similar in colour to alabaster and is rare because of its limited supply.

Today, the village has expanded and become a popular holiday destination for both Maltese and overseas' visitors because it offers spectacular panoramic views. A steep and scenic road leads downhill to the coastline below at Qbajjar Bay and on to the resort town of Marsalforn.

Discovering Malta & Gozo Through its People & Culture

A project initiated by the Ministry for Tourism, the Environment and Culture in 2011 has led to the development of a number of itineraries for villages and towns which are considered to be on the periphery with regard to mainstream tourism, but which nonethelss showcase the real and authentic experience of the Maltese Islands.

Żebbuġ (Gozo) was one of the localities included in the first set of itineraries and maps developed for this project.

Visitor Attractions

Gozo 360

Glorious Gozo! A little island in the sun, concentrated with a fascinating history, rich with crafts, culture and color, an island of charm and joy.

Now, the very essence of Gozo has been captured in a stunning sound and vision experience. More than a thousand color pictures have been combined to create an entertainment which will delight you with its music, legend, tapestry of history and spectacular scenery. In a little under half an hour, we will give you a glimpse of Gozo's past an insight of Gozo of today.

Sit back in air-conditioned comfort, select the commentary language of your choice and be transported across the Gozitan countryside and across the centuries.

A spectacular sound and vision experience which brings the Island to Life.

Gozo 360 - You Have To See It To Believe It!!!!
Languages : Danish Dutch, English, Finnish, French, German, Greek, Hungarian, Japanese, Maltese, Polish, Russian, Spanish, Swedish, Italian and Hebrew.

Magro Food Village

The Magro Brothers firm has been in the food trade in Gozo since 1916. The business started off with three brothers who were provision merchants, bartering Gozitan agricultural produce for products originating on the main island of Malta or abroad. They would travel to Malta twice a week, taking a whole day each time. They would exchange their Gozitan fruit and vegetables for kitchen utensils and whatever else was needed on Gozo. These items were then sold on the market in Pjazza Savina in ir-Rabat (Victoria), which for many centuries was Gozo's main market square.

Tomato processing - a big activity in Gozo

Gozo produces very tasty tomatoes and most of those not eaten fresh are processed by Magro Brothers into cans of pulp, juice, tomato paste and delicious ketchup and sauces..

Cheese-making Centre

Besides the tomato factory, the Magro food village houses a cheese-making centre and a gourmet yoghurt facility. Here Magro Brothers produces cheeses and dairy products using traditional methods (though to modern hygiene standards). The range includes the traditional Gozitan cheeselets (small cheeses), fresh ricotta and excellent Pekorin cheese...really worth a try!

Keeping Mediterranean traditions alive at Savina Creations

Magro is not just a factory and dairy. It is also the home of Savina Creations. Named after Savina Square in Victoria where the early Magro brothers first traded, Savina Foods produces premium Gozitan, Maltese and Mediterranean speciality foods made by hand in the traditional way.

In the Savina Creativity Centre, you can watch artisan foods in the making. Exactly what you see depends on what is being produced that day. It might be Gozitan cheeselets (small cheeses), chutney, sun-dried figs, olive oil, honey or jam. All the products are local specialities and made with only the best ingredients. You will also be able to watch traditional crafts such as lace-making and candlemaking and - most importantly - taste the foods, which can of course also be bought to take home as presents and souvenirs.

Restaurants

Caffino

This popular coffee-spot is a haven for sweet lovers looking for a quick fix. With comfortable indoor or outdoor seating options, Caffino is a sanctuary of tranquillity set back from the busy bay. Grab a quick coffee, indulge in a delectable desert prepared by our specialised pastry team or simply watch the world go by over a cool drink. Open daily.

Dragon Chinese Restaurant

Famed for its Oriental cuisine, Dragon was the first Chinese restaurant to open in Gozo and it deserves its favourable reputation.

Our Chinese chef will prepare authentic dishes to suit your tastes as you enjoy a meal packed with flavour.

Gazebo - Garden Restaurant

For a break in your poolside routine, amble over to the Gazebo, the garden restaurant of the Kempinski Hotel San Lawrenz. The lush and shaded garden surrounds of the Kempinski Hotel San Lawrenz are home to the outdoors-only restaurant Gazebo.

When temperatures soar, a Sicilian Pasta Salad with herb marinated shrimps, orange segments, avocado, broccoli florettes, cherry tomatoes and freh basil makes your day as tasteful as ever. The sheer bliss of holiday life... Relish an ice-chilled chardonnay and watch the soothing play of sunrays filtered through bamboo roofs and the fronds of tall-standing palms.

The Gazebo is open only during the Summer Season.

Il-Baldakkin Café & Lounge

Share a drink with friends or just while away the time with a book at Il-Baldakkin, the Bistro & Lounge of the Kempinski Hotel San Lawrenz.

The versatile Bistro & Lounge of the Kempinski Hotel San Lawrenz, is anything, from a relaxing hub to meet friends over a light meal or just a glass of wine during a beautiful sunset, to a refuge from boredom, an enjoyable extension of your hotel room. Surrender to the temptation of sinfully delicious pastries, sided by an aroma-oozing cuppa - or resign yourself to one of our wickedly delightful cocktails... Try a Kinnie Mojito, which marries Malta's bitter-sweet drink with Cuban rum and cane sugar, refined with a touch of lime and mint leaves from our herb garden - an enthralling mélange of the tastes of Gozo! The west-facing terrace of Il-Baldakkin is a suntrap all the year round, a perfect place to spend the enchanting twilight hour until sunset... In winter spectacular cloudscapes form alliances with the setting sun to deliver dramatic vistas.

Il-Carrubo
This elegant restaurant offers spectacular views of Comino and Malta in beautiful surroundings. The menu consists of a delightful blend of Italian, Maltese, Mediterranean and French cusine.

Mediterranean Breeze
There is no debate about the essential place to be at sundown. It is at the hotel's rooftop bar and restaurant. The spacious Mediterranean Breeze, scorched during the day, is pleasant in the evening. Here one has yet a different perspective of the stunning views enjoyed from this hotel. The Comino watchtower, the silhouette of Malta's northern coast and Fort Chambray form a suggestive frame around the shimmering Mediterranean Sea. Here you can enjoy a fine selection of mouth watering antipasto, live cooking and grill, and theme-dining.

Peppi's Bar

Peppi's Bar is the ideal spot for a lingering pre or post dinner beverage. Our experienced barmen will prepare the best colourful drink for you while pianists and guitarists provide hours of gentle entertainment, helping to make your evening all the more enjoyable.

Sunset

Situated on the roof terrace, the Sunset Bar is the ideal location to enjoy a drink or a light meal. This venue is situated on Hotel Calypso's rooftop where one can enjoy the panoramic bay and country views. Our bar is stocked with premium wines, spirits and beers while our snack menu offers tasty options which can be enjoyed by the poolside.

Guests will surely enjoy the restaurant's tranquil environment and elegant ambience. The restaurant opens daily for lunch and dinner during the summer season. We would like to inform you that non-residents are also welcomed!

So why not indulge yourself at Hotel Calypso's sundeck and watch the panoramic views while grabbing a snack or sipping a cocktail.

The Lounge Bar

The clientele in the Lounge Bar is a mixture of locals and foreigners. Hotel guests can relax inside in the air-conditioned area, sip on a drink or savor some of the appetizing items on the snack menu, or move outdoor to the bar terrace and absorb the cacophony produced by harbour activity down the road.

Trattoria San Lawrenz

At the Trattoria San Lawrenz, our chef conjures delightful dishes inspired by our neighbour country, Italy.

Surrounded by warm colours and vaulted ceilings, a dinner at the Italian-inspired Trattoria San Lawrenz is an informal yet stylish affair, topped up with a generous pinch of vacation spirit. Among the items vying for your attention on the varied menu of the Trattoria San Lawrenz, you'll find a delicious assortment of pasta and risottos and other genuine Italian fare. Try our Oreccietti pasta with fresh sea urchins and Parmesan foam and Bresaola with fig salad and fresh goat cheese! Freshly caught fish is available all the year round, cooked to the chef's inspiration - or your own wishes

Zafiro Restaurant

The Zafiro Restaurant is located on the Xlendi seafront stretching onto the promenade having picture postcard views of the bay. Tranquil and peaceful, turquoise waters lap the sandy shore exuding an air of charm and character. The Zafiro restaurant specializes in local and Mediterranean cuisine serving indoors or al fresco on its beautiful terrace.

The a La Carte menu offers a mouth-watering variety of fresh pasta, antipasti, an exquisite selection of fresh fish, shellfish, lobster, freshly grilled premium quality steaks and other various other meat dishes. An impressive choice of local and foreign wines can be selected from the extensive wine list.

The Zafiro Restaurant also prides itself of freshly home-baked desserts such as its well known banoffee pie to finish off a perfect meal.

Arzella Restaurant
Treat yourself to a magnificent seafood dinner at sunset or unwind over a relaxing lunch whilst enjoying breathtaking views of sun and sea. Sample crisp fruity wines as an accompaniment to mouth-watering Mediterranean cuisine, from our house speciality mixed fish platter of freshly caught fish an shellfish, to tasty aromatic pastas, meat, chicken and an ever-changing list of specials, loving prepared by our chef with the freshest ingredients. All this and more may be enjoyed at Ristorante Arzella, where our staff will be

more than happy to serve you and ensure a truly positive dining experience.

D Bar & Restaurant

D-BAR is a family run Restaurant, Pizzeria and Bar. Brimming with charm and tradition, one finds themselves at the bar and dining area with surrounding field's names covering the walls of the lower level. On the other hand, the upper level has a different setting and style, boasting a collection of old style photographs of Qala. Moreover, one can find a nice terrace which diners can use in the summer months.

The food at D-BAR has been termed as fabulous by the various patrons who return time and time again. It is prepared with great zeal by Twanny and Natalie, the owners, and his darling mother Cetta, together with Sunny the Nephew.

The food is always freshly prepared. We do not believe in half cooking and warming up. Whatever you order is always prepared there and then. You may have to wait some time but your patience will surely be rewarded!!

Il Forno Tavern

The setting is an exceptional house of character in front of the sea dating back to 1700 AD. This is the oldest historic dwelling in the village with robust traditional stone walls. The ground floor has been maintained to its original state whilst the first floor was designed and built by the owner to complement the original.

This establishment specialises in exquisite Italian and Maltese Cuisine, although one or two Chinese items are also included for good measure.

Interestingly the owner is renowned for his many natural talents and often picks up a guitar filling the place with beautiful Brazilian or Swing music which, in addition to the very reasonable prices and handsome portions which characterise this restaurant, makes your outing simply unique.

Il-Panzier Restaurant

Il-Panzier Restaurant has managed against all the odds to become successful restaurant serving typical Sicilian fare. The owner, Valentino took it on after a series of mishaps, embarking on a new business in a foreign country, with a restaurant that had been abandoned twice in a row and lost its clientele. With acumen and verve, Valentino managed the place back to success serving genuine food with the help of Alexandra who has taken over the kitchen.

Even though Il-Panzier is situated in a quiet location in Gozo, it has managed to entice clients with its selection of fresh meats, fresh fish and typical genuine Sicilian ingredients such as extra virgin olive oil and delicious seasonal products.

This family-run business enjoys easy parking on two nearby squares. The restaurant also comes with its own private garden with special accessibility for wheel-chair users. Staff members speak five different languages and the menu itself is set in five different languages. Eat from hand-designed plates, each one is different from rest. Sit at tables made of Sicilian ceramic and lava stone from Mount Etna. Eat exquisite Sicilian dishes. Immerse yourself in a Sicilian experience at Il-Panzier.

Patrick's Tmun Restaurant
Welcome to Patrick's...
where we are delighted to be of service to you. For many years, we have worked hard and are very pleased to report that we have successfully achieved a reputation as one of the foremost restaurants in Malta & Gozo.

Our a' la carte menu features dishes to suit all tastes and we have again been awarded one of the top 40 rated restaurants for the quality of our food and service by The Definitive(ly) Good Guide to Restaurants

Porto Vecchio

Porto Vecchio Ristorante e Vinoteca ....Where it is always our pleasure to be of service to you and our delight to make your lunch or dinner a relaxed and enjoyable occasion. We have been open since June 2007 and we can proudly say that our reputation has been growing steadily. We are now considered as one of the foremost restaurants on the Islands, thanks to the support of our clients.

We are situated on the seafront at the yacht marina in Mgarr, where one can enjoy the beautiful and peaceful surroundings of Mgarr Harbour whilst savouring lunch or dinner right on the water's edge.Enjoy the best Mediterranean cuisine, prepared from the finest ingredients which we import directly from the Friuli region in Italy, such as, goose, kidd and venison salamis, speck di sauris, prosciutto San Daniele, air-dried loin of pork (Lonza di Maiale), air-dried breast of duck and a variety of cheeses.

Our varied menu of antipasto, soups, pasta, fresh fish and meat is prepared with passion by our chef and his team, the Italian way "alla buona", to be enjoyed with a nice bottle of wine from our extensive selection available. Flambe' cooking by one's table and fresh fish are our speciality. A list of our daily specialities is available with the Al A'Carte menu. A summer light meals menu is also available. Be it a Sunday lunch, a special occasion or just an evening out, enjoy the comfortable, warm and friendly atmosphere that our restaurant offers.

Salvina Restaurant

We are situated in one of the most tranquil and picturesque villages of Gozo - the peaceful villlage of Għarb, host of the magnificent cathedral of Ta' Pinu surrounded by breath taking countrysides like the Wied il-Mielaħ which ends at Marsalforn.

Ta' Salvina restaurant can hold 50 persons, specialises on fresh local fish, but also includes meat and poultry dishes. The real treat is rabbit cooked in the traditional local recipe. Not to forget a number of vegetarian and pasta dishes.

Sofia.

Sofia Bar & Restaurant is the first Balkan restaurant on the island of Gozo. Sofia restaurant offers dishes mainly from Bulgaria, Greece and Turkey, to accompany a selection of wines (mainly Bulgarian, local wines are also available).

Sofia restaurant are trying to offer a different concept by being different in every field; Food - the best real salads, fresh grill meat, homemade dishes available everyday (like Musaka and stuffed peppers, amongst others), homemade pitta bread (which is given to every customer free of charge), homemade desserts and seafood dishes which are presented and cooked according to traditional Balkan styles.

We would also like to inform our customers that the following can be ordered one day in advance: whole baby pig, chicken, fish, lamb capama, all cooked the traditional Balkan way.

Ta' Frenc

The Restaurant is an authentic old farmhouse. It is surrounded by beautiful country views of Xagħra, Żebbuġ and Maraslforn valley. Over the years there have been various improvements in order to make the restaurant more comfortable.

Ta' Frenc is the perfect show case for chef Mario Schembri's award-winning cooking, which is what makes dining at Ta' Frenc so special. His techniques as a classically-trained chef combined with a sensitive appreciation of Maltese culinary traditions and a vivid awareness of the contemporary kitchen produce food at Ta'Frenc which satisfies the most discerning and well-travelled diner; his rabbit ravioli, for example, is internationally renowned.

The chef and owners have been determined to maintain a strong culinary identity at Ta' Frenc, rather than offering a 'global village' menu, so that visitors to Ta' Frenc would know that they were on Gozo and could experience its regional distinctiveness on the plate

Anthony's Restaurant
Situated in Gozo's popular village of Nadur and located just behind the church of Nadur is the delightful restaurant and wine bar Anthony's.

Food-wise, Anthony's menu offers a selection of soups, salads, pasta, meat, fish, burgers and pizza. Some superbly dishes include 'Gozitan Platter', 'Aaron's Pasta', 'Rib Eye', 'Fish Platter', 'Anthony's Burger' and 'Pjazzetta'. Either tuck into the wine list or choose from the admirable assortment or beers or have them mix you up a cocktail. Enjoy the evening in the lovely village of the Nadur at Anthony's

Arzella Restaurant
Treat yourself to a magnificent seafood dinner at sunset or unwind over a relaxing lunch whilst enjoying breathtaking views of sun and

sea. Sample crisp fruity wines as an accompaniment to mouth-watering Mediterranean cuisine, from our house speciality mixed fish platter of freshly caught fish an shellfish, to tasty aromatic pastas, meat, chicken and an ever-changing list of specials, loving prepared by our chef with the freshest ingredients. All this and more may be enjoyed at Ristorante Arzella, where our staff will be more than happy to serve you and ensure a truly positive dining experience.

Vineyards

Ta' Mena Estate

At Ta' Mena Estate, you will find yourself immersed in the typical Gozitan country-side, surrounded by a natural and calm environment, and breathtaking views : Malta's sister is characterised by its peaceful and rural environment, signs of quality and tradition.

The Estate is situated in the picturesque Marsalforn Valley between Victoria and Marsalforn Bay. It includes a fruit garden, an olive grove with about 1500 olive trees, an orange grove, and over 10 hectares of vineyards. It enjoys the panoramic views of the Gozo Citadel and the surrounding hills and villages.

We offer a large range of local products such as our Traditional Kunserva Tomato Paste, Pure Gozo Honey, Jams, Cheeses, Pates, and our Cold Pressed Extra Virgin Olive Oil. Most of the fruits, olives, herbs and vegetables come from our Estate, and they are all produced using traditional methods and slow cooking with natural ingredients only.

We also produce wines, characterised by the "Island Effect" in our state-of-art winery and made from our Gozitan estate vines. Our blends have been certified as GOZO D.O.K. Wines, the highest wine certification in Malta. We insure a strict control of the process from the vine to the bottle by practicing rigid green pruning, traditional methods in the vineyards and the best wine producing practices.

Through Ta' Mena Estate, you will learn about our wines and food processing, symbol of our Gozitan culture and family traditions.

At Ta' Mena Estate we organise different activities such as guided tours around the estate followed by wine and food tasting, lunches and dinners, barbecues, snacks, cooking sessions, full/half day activities, etc. We also offer agricultural experiences including fruit picking, wine-making, olive-oil pressing and more.

Moreover, here at Ta' Mena, we set up the Estate so we can host anniversary and birthday receptions, conferences, weddings and other functions... with a green touch ! The catering for any of these occasions can be provided by our team.

The estate offers a unique holiday, far away from the complicated and stressful daily life of the modern era. You will relax and revitalize yourself while savoring some of the Mediterranean history and nature at its best.

More than our products, this is the passion for our profession but also our land that we want to share : Gozo has so much to offer. Come and enjoy the Gozitan experience !

Tal-Massar Winery
Get an authentic experience of Gozo's life.

TAL-MASSAR family run boutique winery conducts vineyard tours and wine-tasting sessions.

What to expect?
1. Meet us and share our passion in the cultivation of our vines and the production of our wines.
2. Tour our private estate and enjoy the breathtaking views of the medieval village of Gharb.

3. Taste 4 different wines and 3 authentic Gozitan finger foods namely traditional galletti, Gozitan sheep cheese and traditional bread with sundried tomatoes and cold press Gozitan olive oil.

Wedding Venues
Maxtura Ivory Suite & Terrace
The Maxtura Ivory Suite and Terrace is set in the limits of Marsalforn - Gozo. The terrace setting gives unobstructed views of Gozo's picturesque landscape and its surroundings.

The rustic warm décor enhances the Gozitan characteristics whilst the newly renovated Ivory suite compliments elegancy and luxury to your event which makes it an ideal venue for your wedding.

Ta' Frenċ
Planning the most important day of your life is no small matter. The Ta' Frenc Group of Companies excels itself in providing all the essential ingredients for a successful wedding. At Ta' Frenc we can help you make sure everything runs like clockwork. Whether you are planning a reception for 200 guests, or a smaller intimate celebration, we can provide the perfect surroundings. From the moment we receive your enquiry at Ta' Frenc, our dedicated wedding coordinator will oversee every detail from beginning to

end, to ensure that your special day is truly memorable. Our experienced and professional staff will guide you through the many necessary preparations and help with flowers, your wedding cake, place cards, printed menus and limousines. And our special Honeymoon Package of one night's accommodation, Ta' Frenc Champagne, fruit and flowers on arrival is surely the perfect end to the perfect day.

Hold your reception or even the ceremony itself at Ta' Frenc, and you are guaranteed the most perfect wedding imaginable. A choice of reception areas in a choice of styles; select from the sumptuous Wine Cellar, or the restored Executive Dining Room. The Garden, one of the best outside locations surrounded by exceptional country views is ideal for a summer reception.

Bring us your vision and let us show you its realisation. From intimate to extravagant, traditional to unexpected, Ta' Frenc is at your service and dedicated to creating an unforgettable wedding experience that is uniquely yours.

Ta' Mena

Ta' Mena Estate is owned by the Spiteri family namely Joseph, Margaret, Philip, Mark and Patrick together with their father Frank.

The estate was founded by our late mother Carmela, popularly known as Mena, who worked hard to purchase and cultivate the land until her pre-mature death in 1986, when the project was partially shelved.

In 2002 the Spiteri Family decided to start again to regenerate the 25 hectares of agricultural land which used to be a fruit and vegetable garden, to realize their late mother's dream of integrating agriculture with tourism so that one sector sustains the other. After seven years of very intensive planning and hard work, this project is taking shape and should be fully finished in the next two years.

The strategy behind this project is to offer a product with a difference to our clients. We think that too many entities are selling the same product which consists only of the sun, sea and comfort. At Ta' Mena Estate we want to offer more of what is unique to Gozo with its history, folklore and culture.

We want our guests to go around and be taught about crops, trees and food processing in the traditional way. We want to provide a health farm and an educational experience to young children, adolescents and adults. Agri-tourism is definitely the new type of holiday making that is flourishing everywhere and we are sure that

Ta' Mena Estate will be a very particular experience with a Gozitan Green Touch.

Gozo Events

Like its larger sister island of Malta, Gozo offers a colourful annual calendar of traditional seasonal events, including its very own distinct carnival and a number of summer festas. Every year, an eclectic blend of local and international events, entertainment and exhibitions take place.

The island is renowned for the passion and enthusiasm that the locals have for opera. Two theatres located within a few metres of each other in the capital Victoria stage popular favourites by Verdi, Puccini and others to packed houses. Many afficionados travel from Malta and beyond to attend, but finding a seat could be challenging - so early booking is advised.

The island also plays host to a variety of sports championships and tournaments, with football and horseracing being the most popular.

Meet in Gozo

Gozo is renowned as the mythical island of Calypso, who drew Homer's hero Ulysses to its shores for a seven-year hiatus. Though there are only five kilometres of sea between Malta and Gozo, the islands are distinctly different from each other. Gozo is a third of the size of Malta, more rural and tranquil, greener, less bustling but still full of life.

While authentic houses of character have been renovated to suit the most exigent contemporary clients are the speciality of Gozo, the Island also has luxurious hotels. The size and natural setting of the island conspire to make it a prime location for high-powered board meetings, small conferences, workshops and incentives.

Gozo is a must-visit location. It is almost always included in delegates' social programmes as well as pre and post conference leisure-time arrangements. It is particularly renowned for team-building events, dinners, barbeques, active day tours and outdoor events. Moreover, the Island is a conference and incentive destination in its own right, and has the facilities to prove it.

Gozo's colours and flavours are brought out by the radiant skies above it and the blue sea which surrounds its spectacular coast, which is simply waiting to be discovered. Few destinations radiate the warm, magical charm of Gozo. Even fewer can effortlessly blend work with pleasure, in a setting which is peaceful and intriguing at once.

Comino

Situated between Malta and Gozo, the smaller island of Comino is a paradise for snorkelers, divers, windsurfers and ramblers.

Only 3.5 square kilometers, Comino is car-free and apart from one hotel, is virtually uninhabited.

The island's main attraction is the Blue Lagoon. In summer, this sheltered inlet of shimmering aquamarine water over white sand is very popular with day-trippers. Other beaches on the island include Santa Marija Bay and San Niklaw Bay.

Comino is also worth a visit in winter, and is ideal for walkers and photographers. With no urban areas or cars on the island, one can easily smell the scent of wild thyme and other herbs.

Comino was inhabited in the Roman period, but did not have much significance until the Knights arrived. It then had a dual role: hunting grounds and a staging post in the defence of the Maltese Islands against the Ottoman Turks.

The island had proved a useful base for pirates operating in the central Mediterranean and, though stark and barren today, it was home to wild boar and hares when the Knights arrived in 1530. The

Grandmasters went to great lengths to ensure that their game on Comino was protected: anyone found breaking the embargo on hunting could expect to serve three years rowing on a galley.

After WWII, Comino remained a backwater until its fortunes revived with tourism in the mid-1960s.

Where to Stay
Comino has one resort hotel, which is ideal for those looking for a tranquil getaway.

www.ingramcontent.com/pod-product-compliance
Lightning Source LLC
Chambersburg PA
CBHW021108080526
44587CB00010B/437